Cute Animal Coloring Book *for* *Girls*

This Book

Belongs To

....

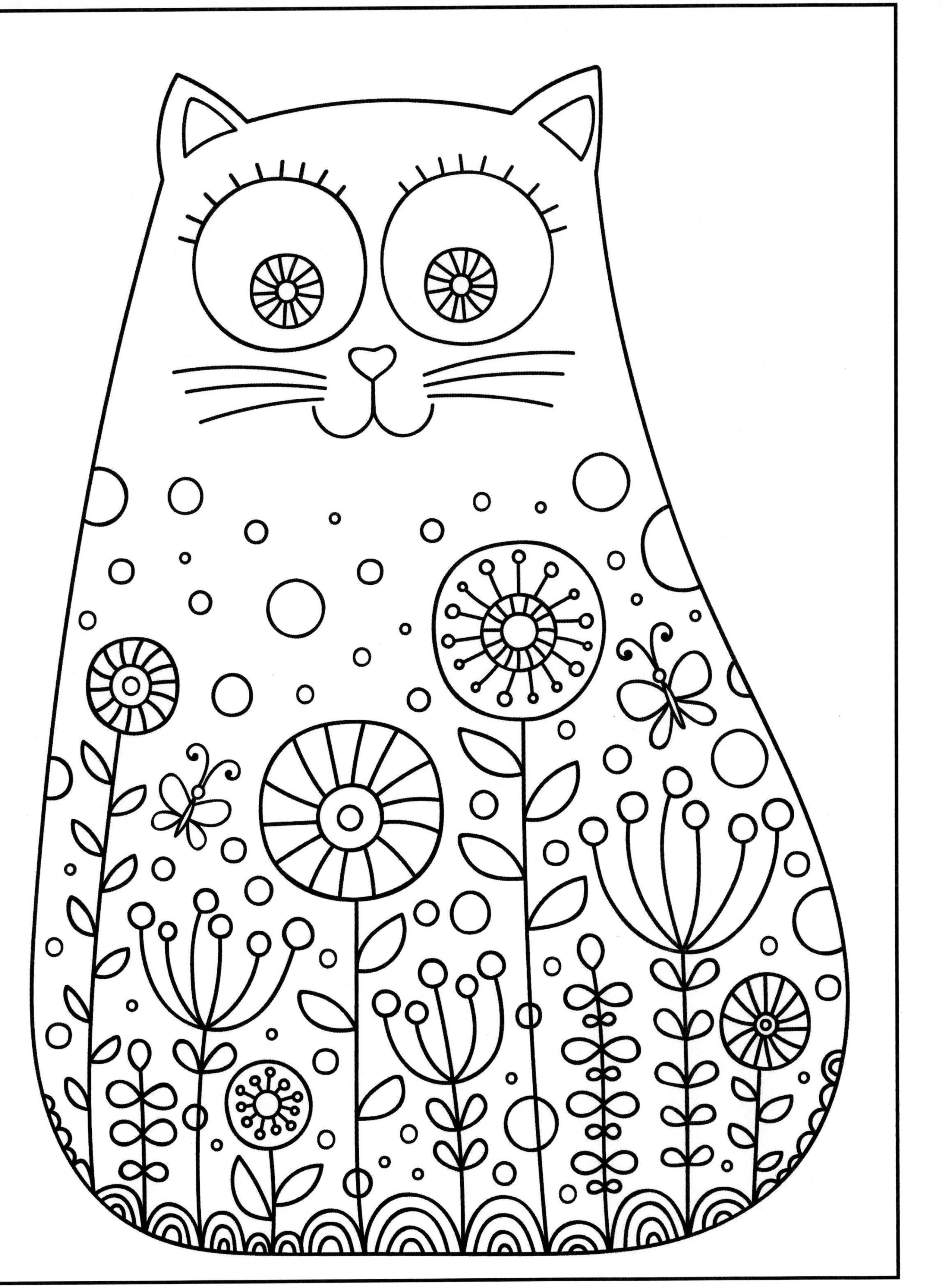

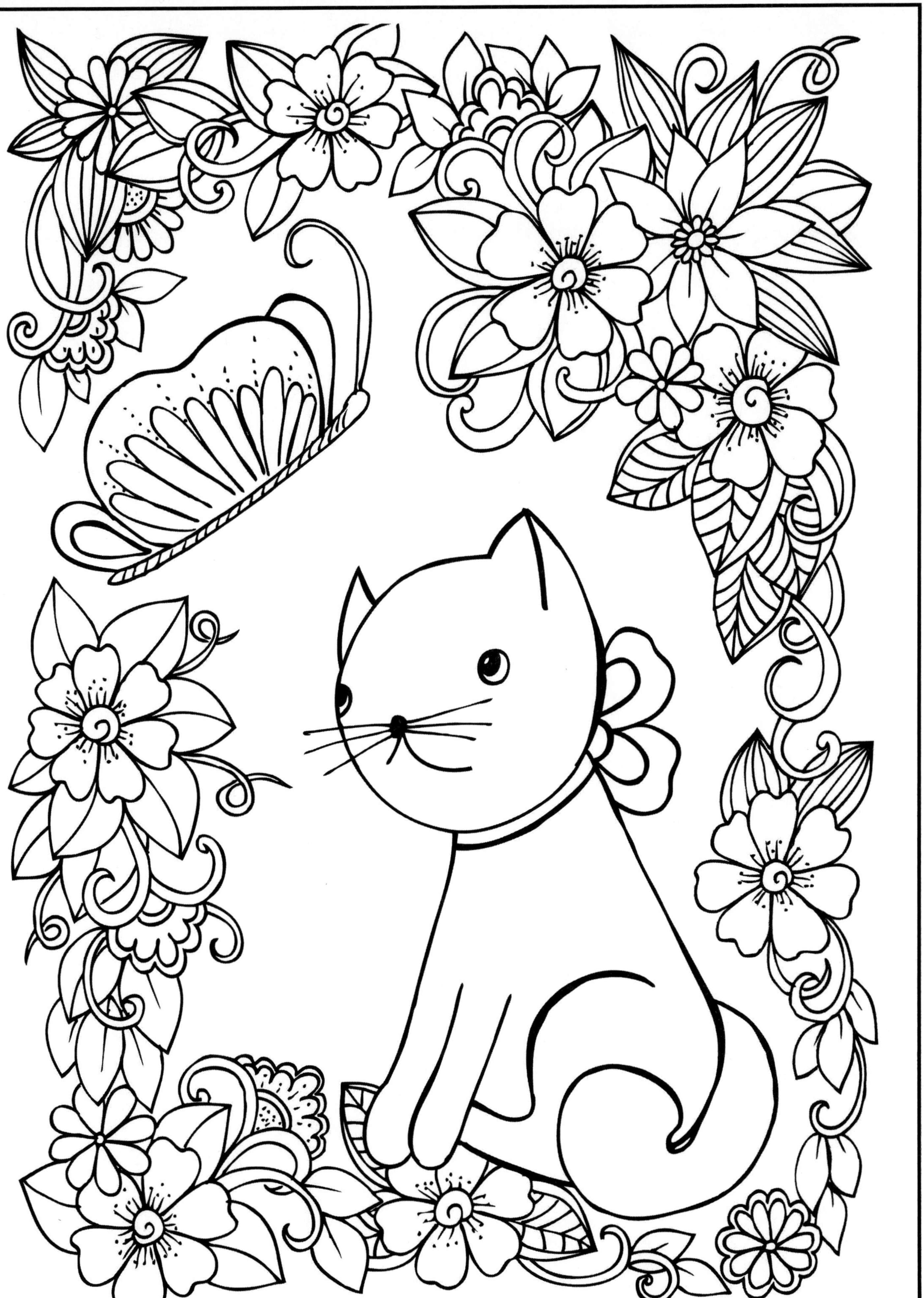

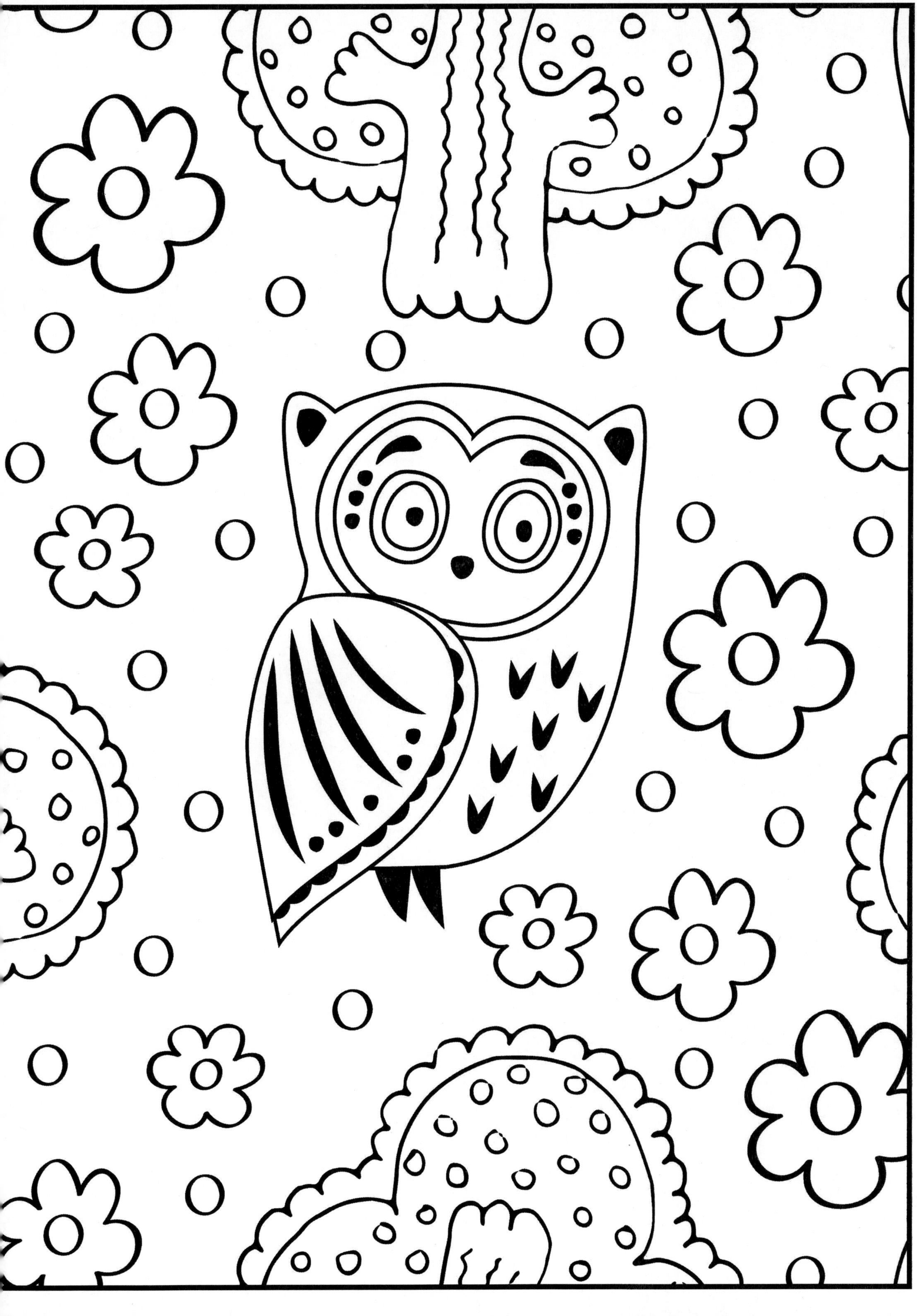

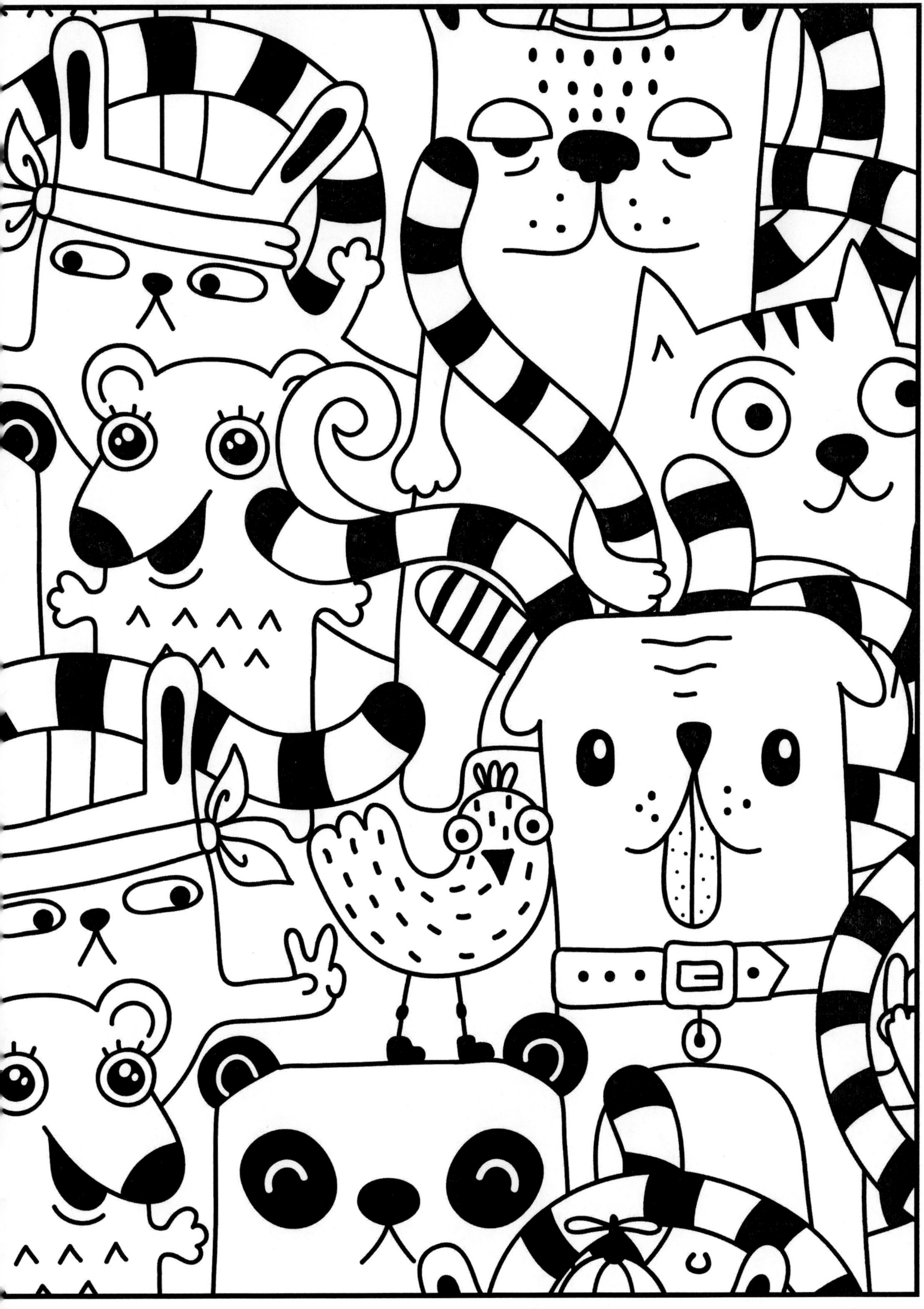

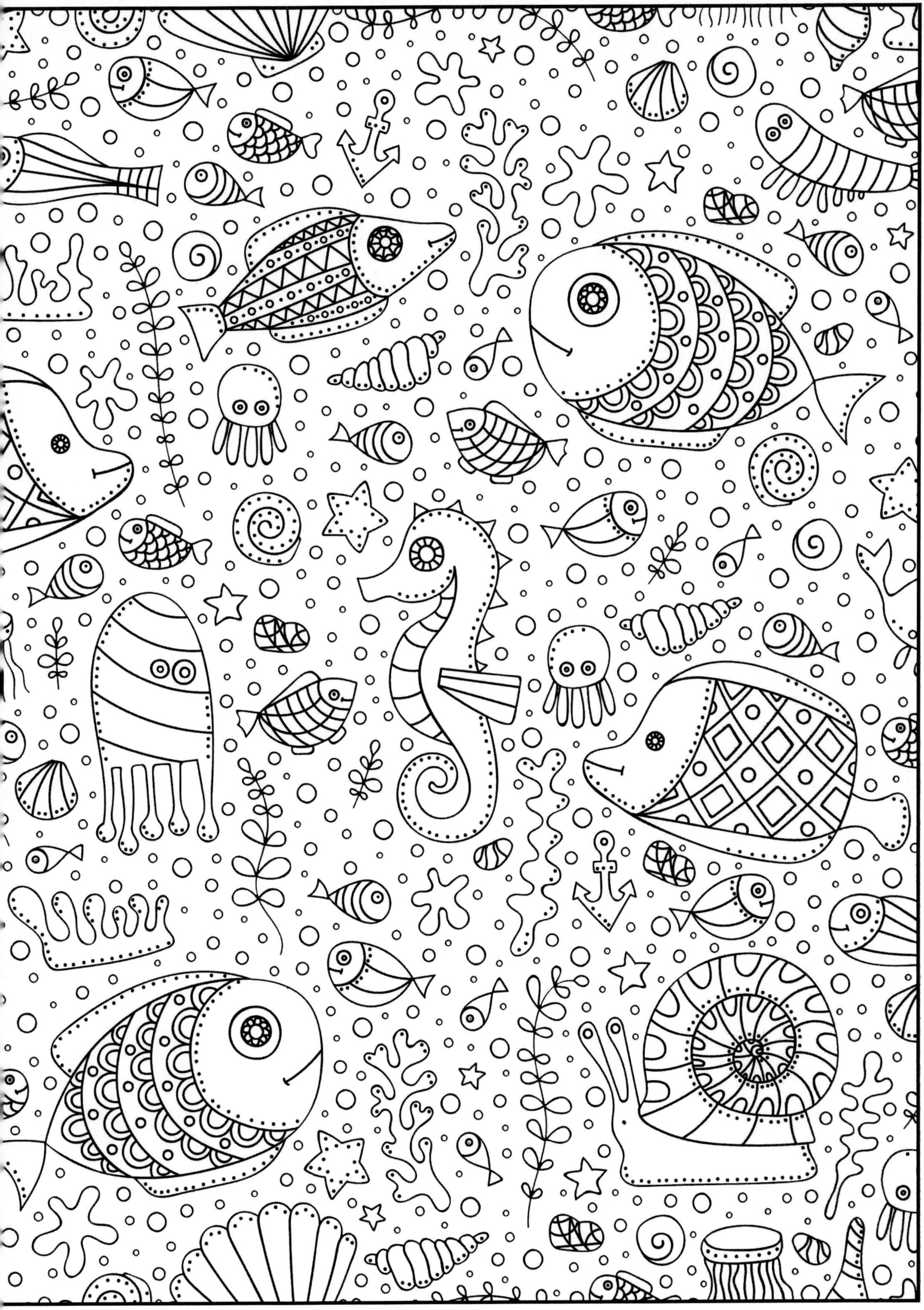

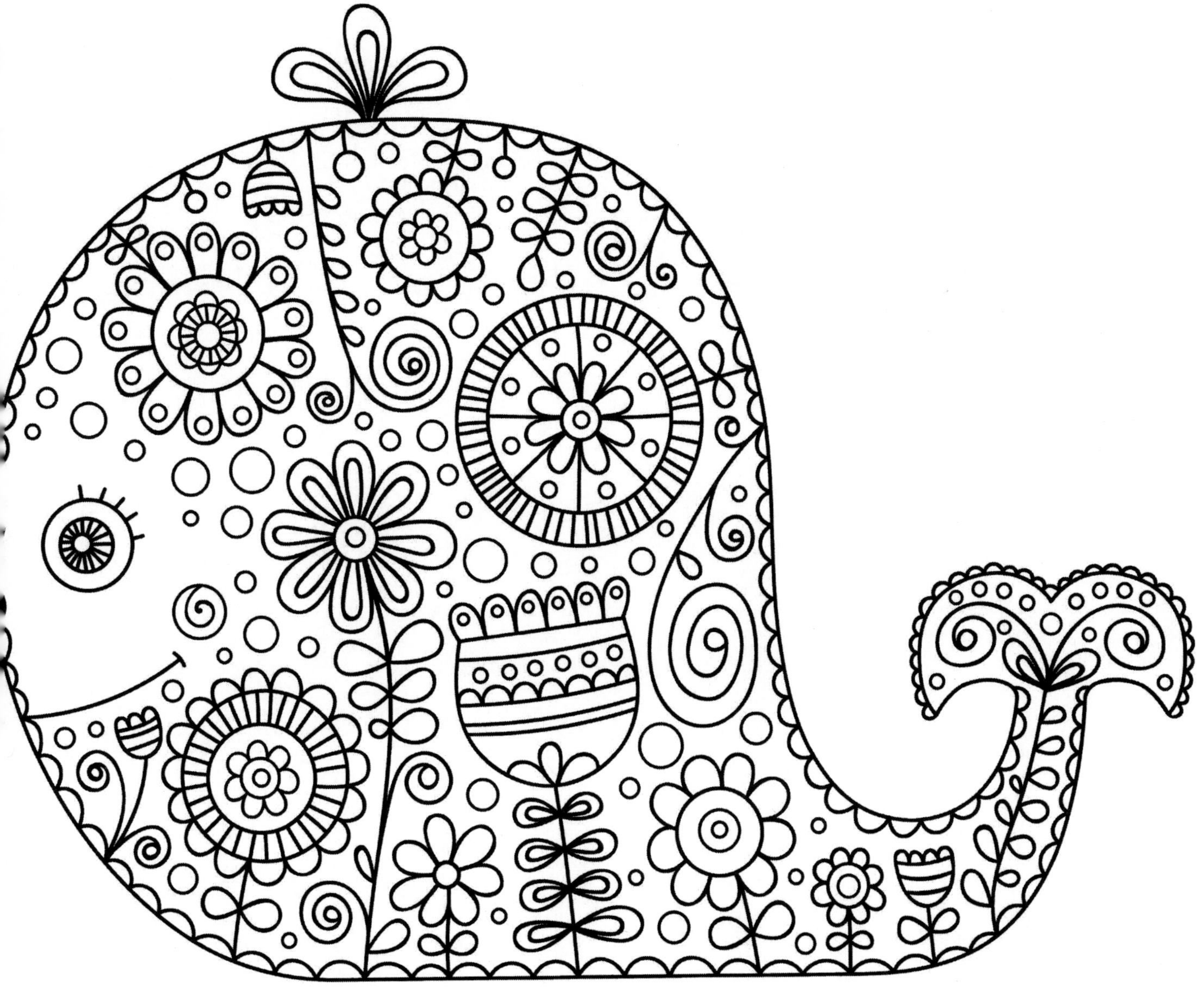

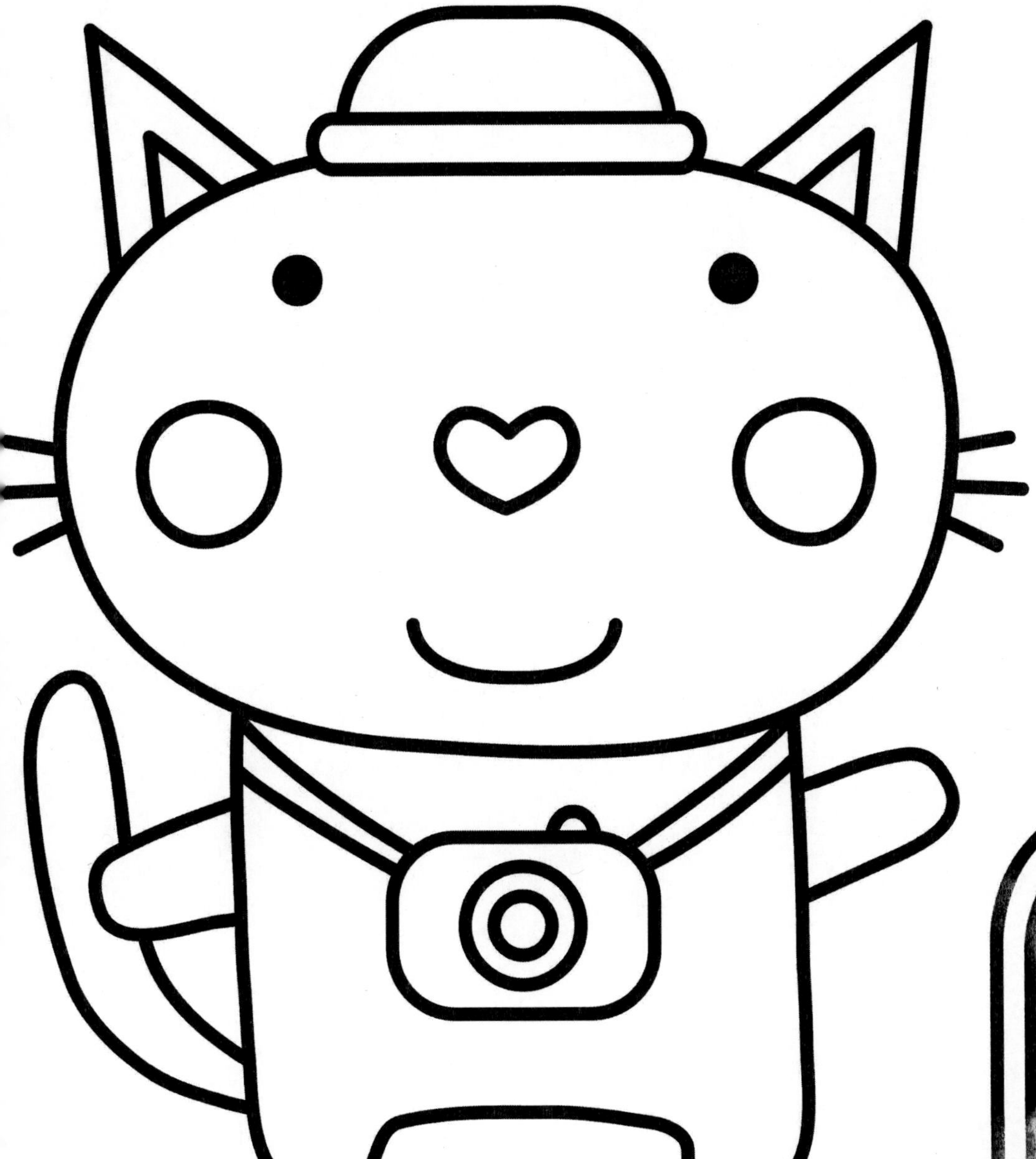

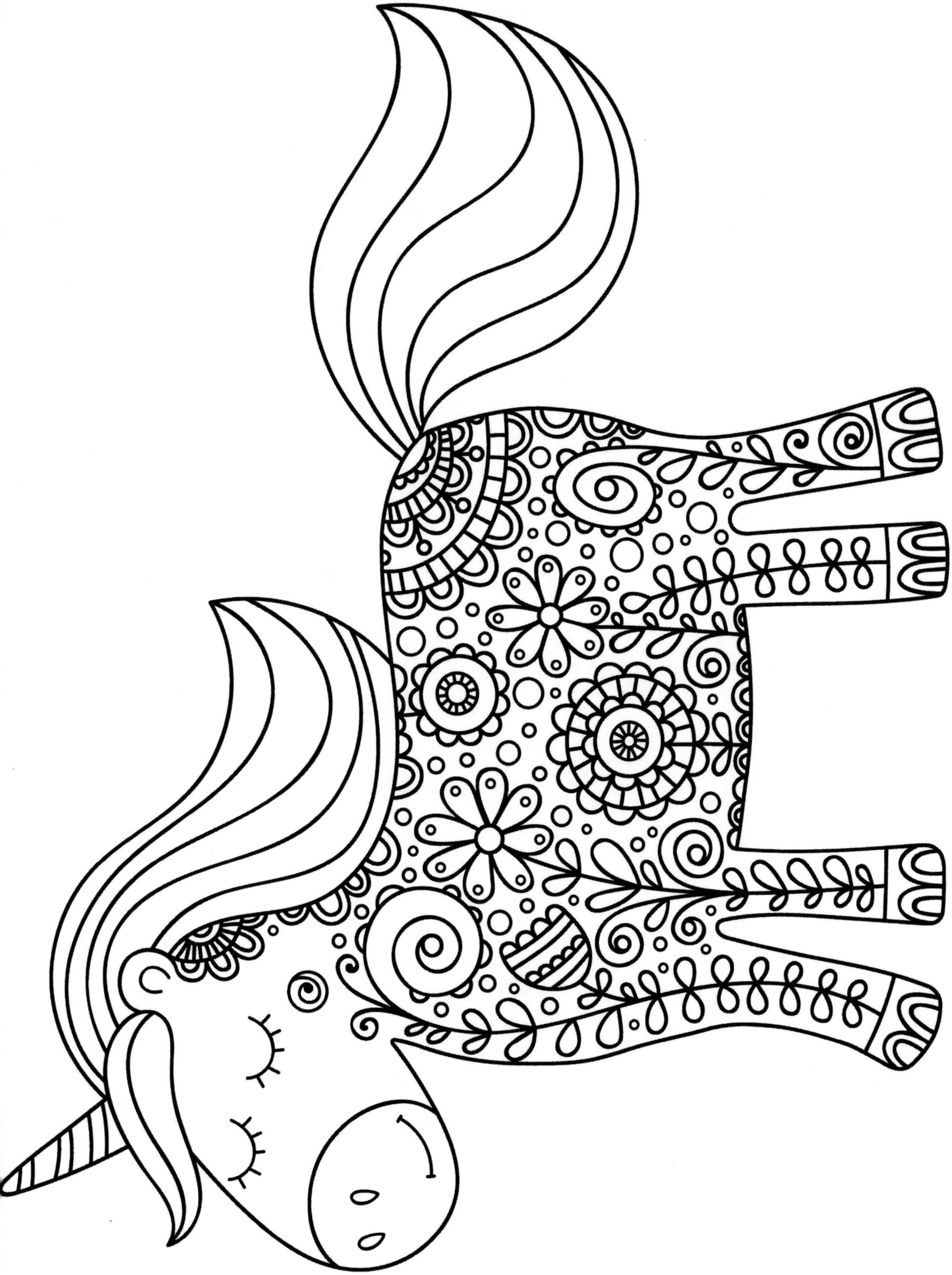

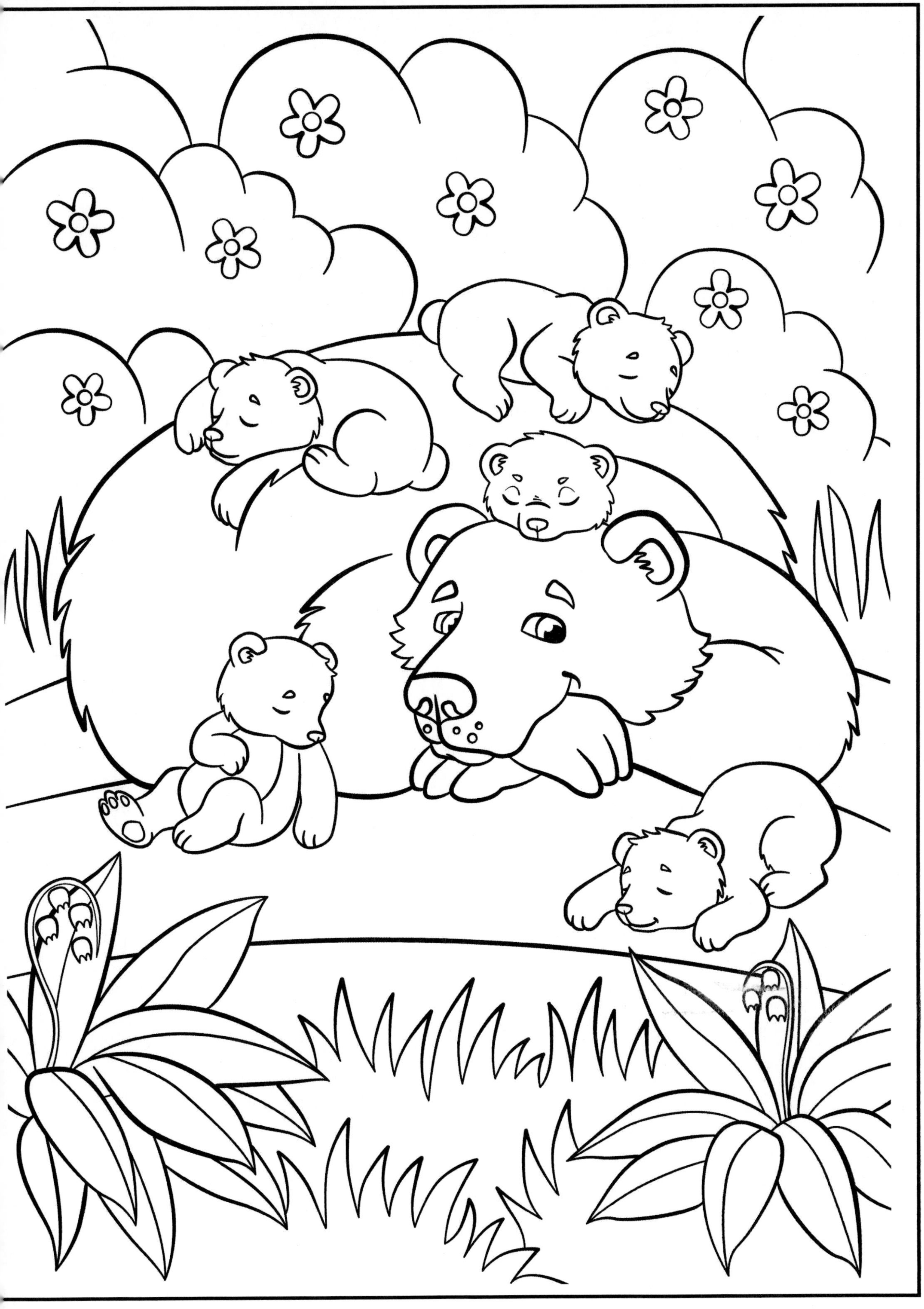

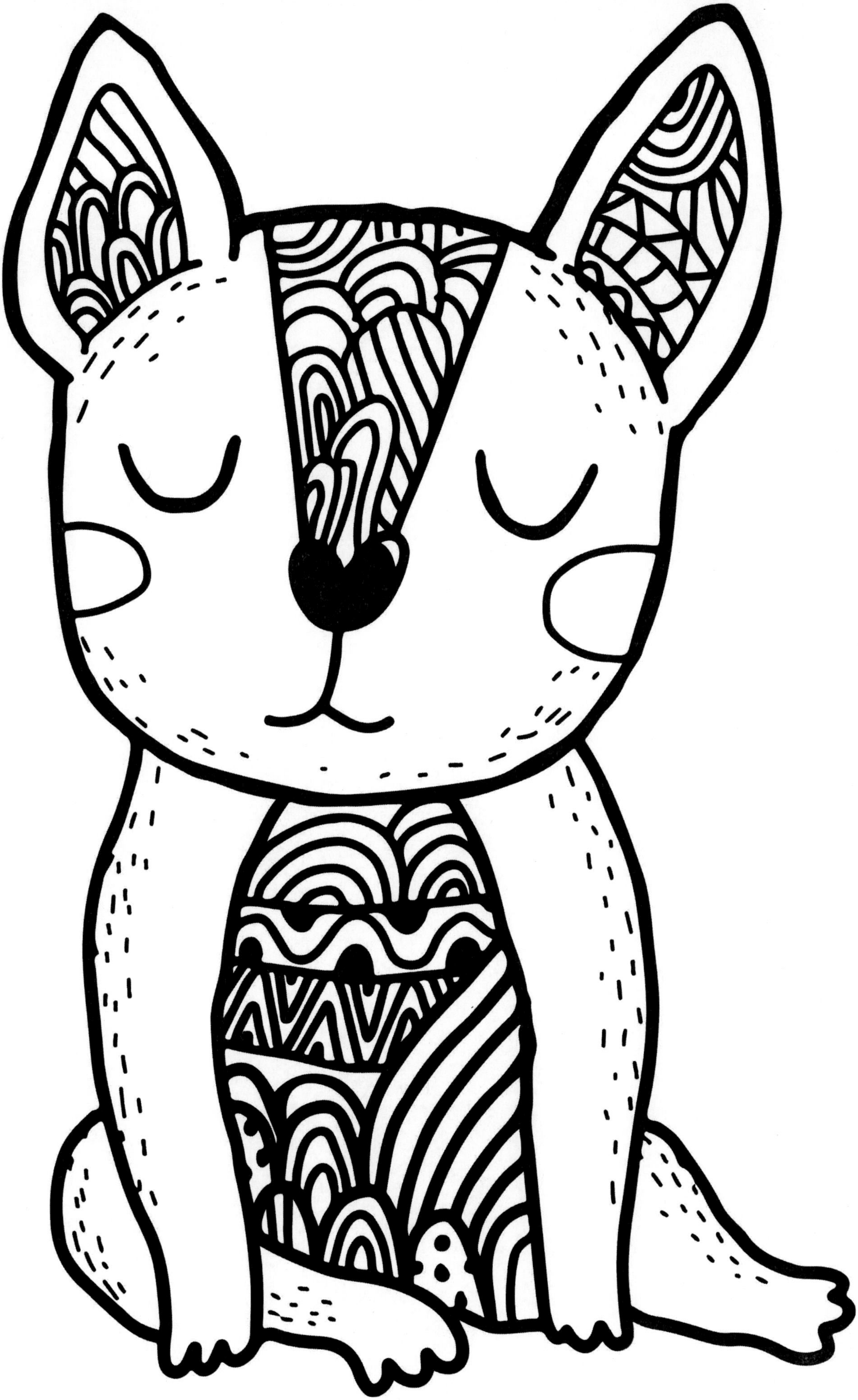

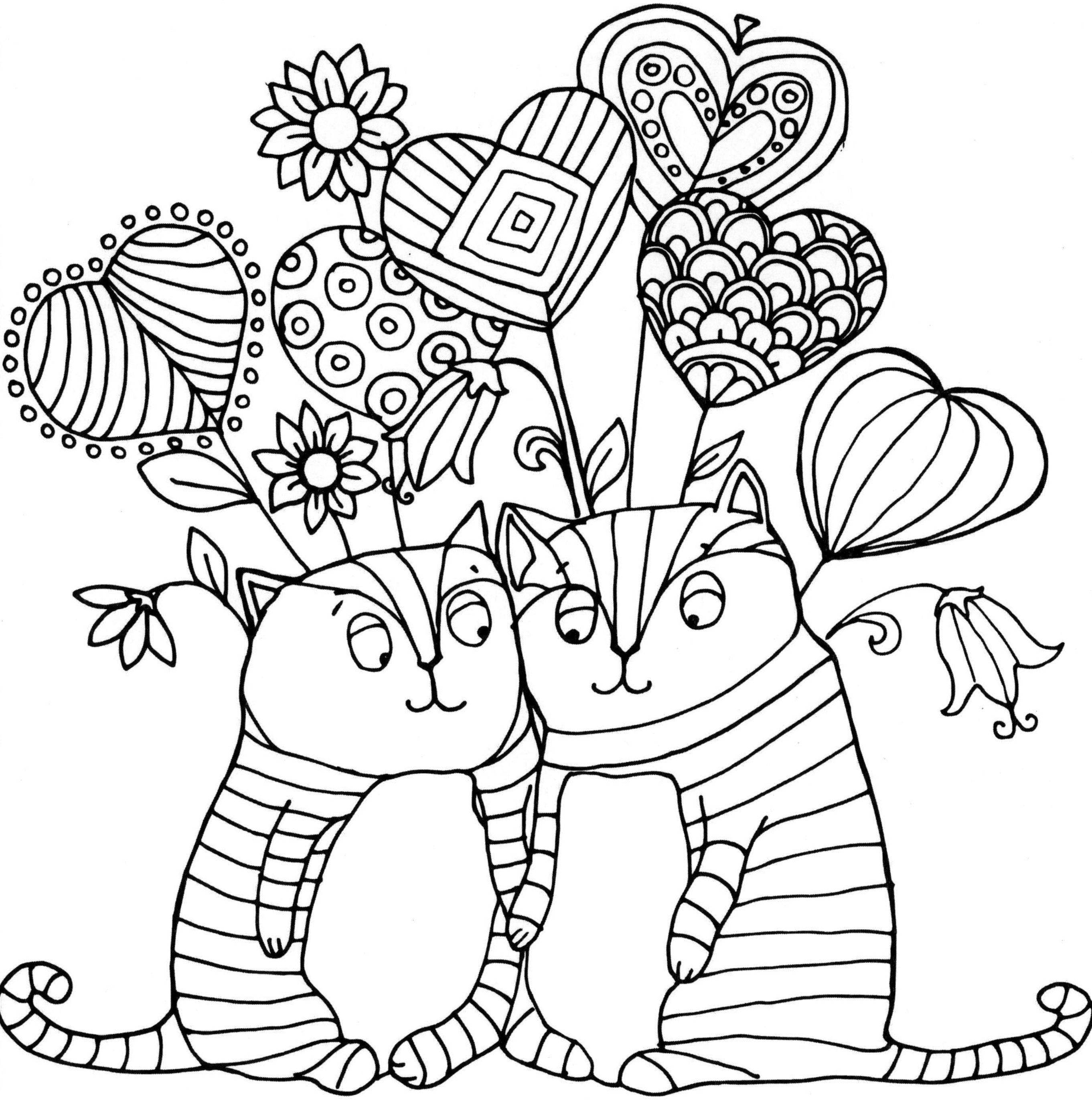

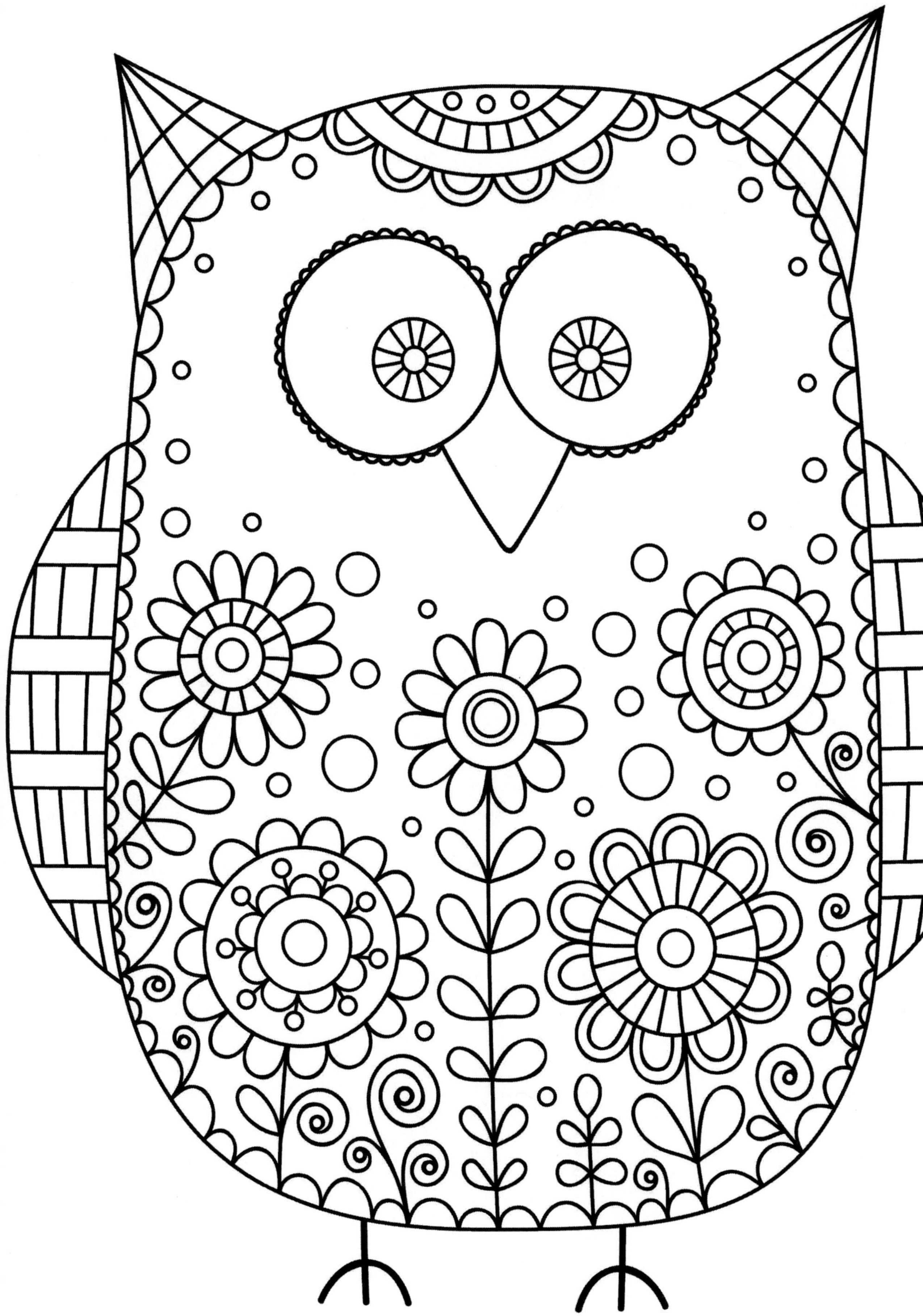

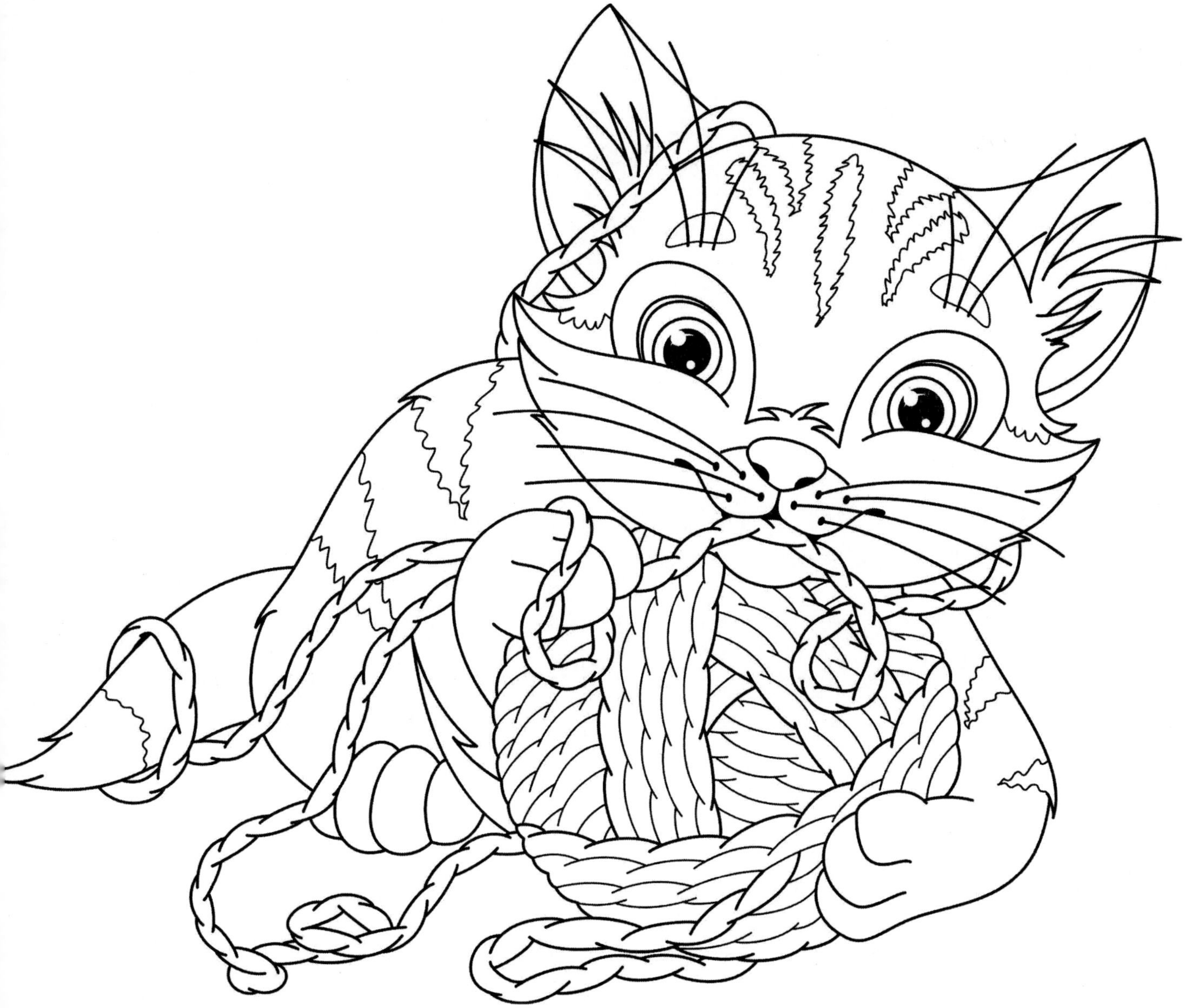

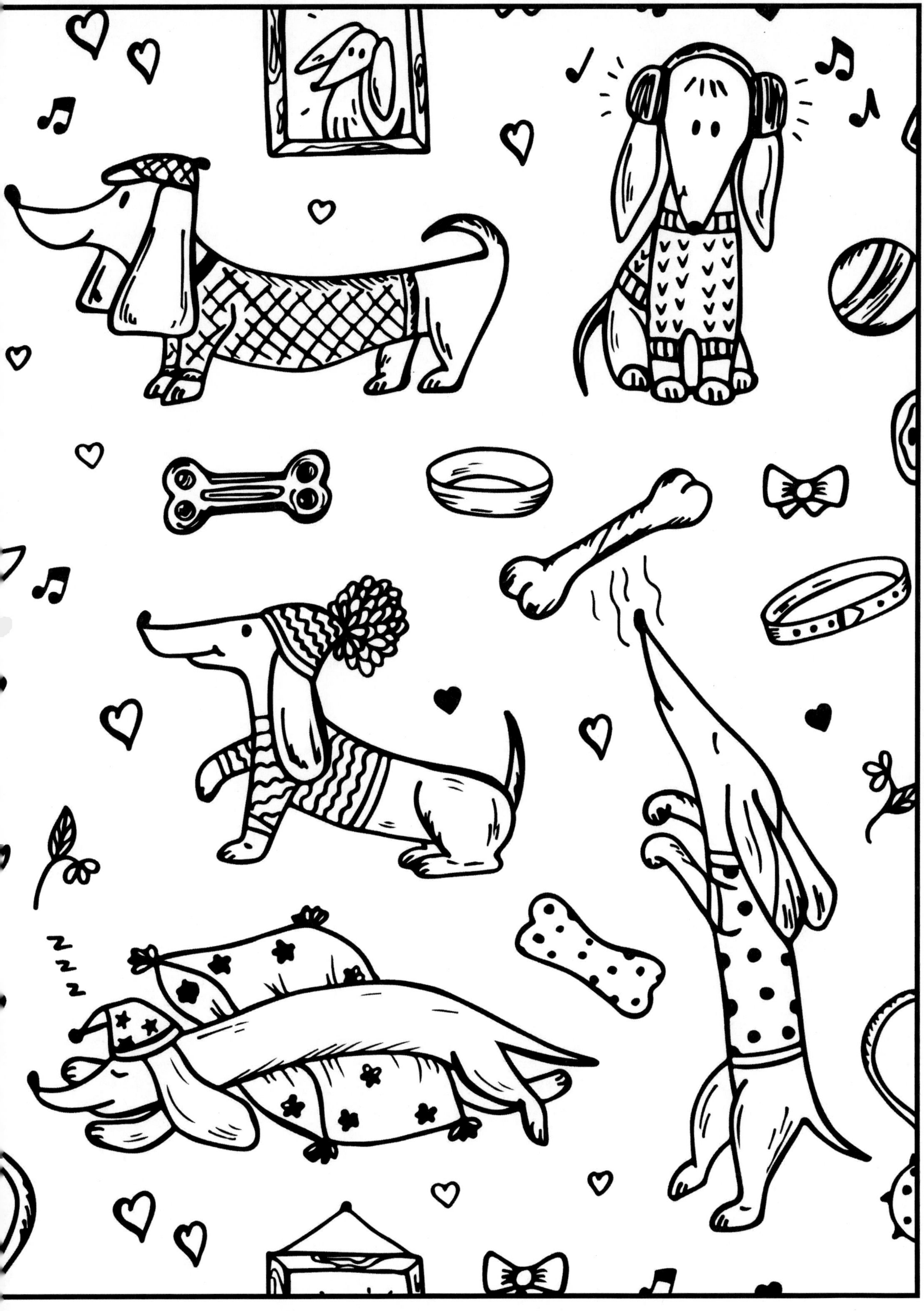

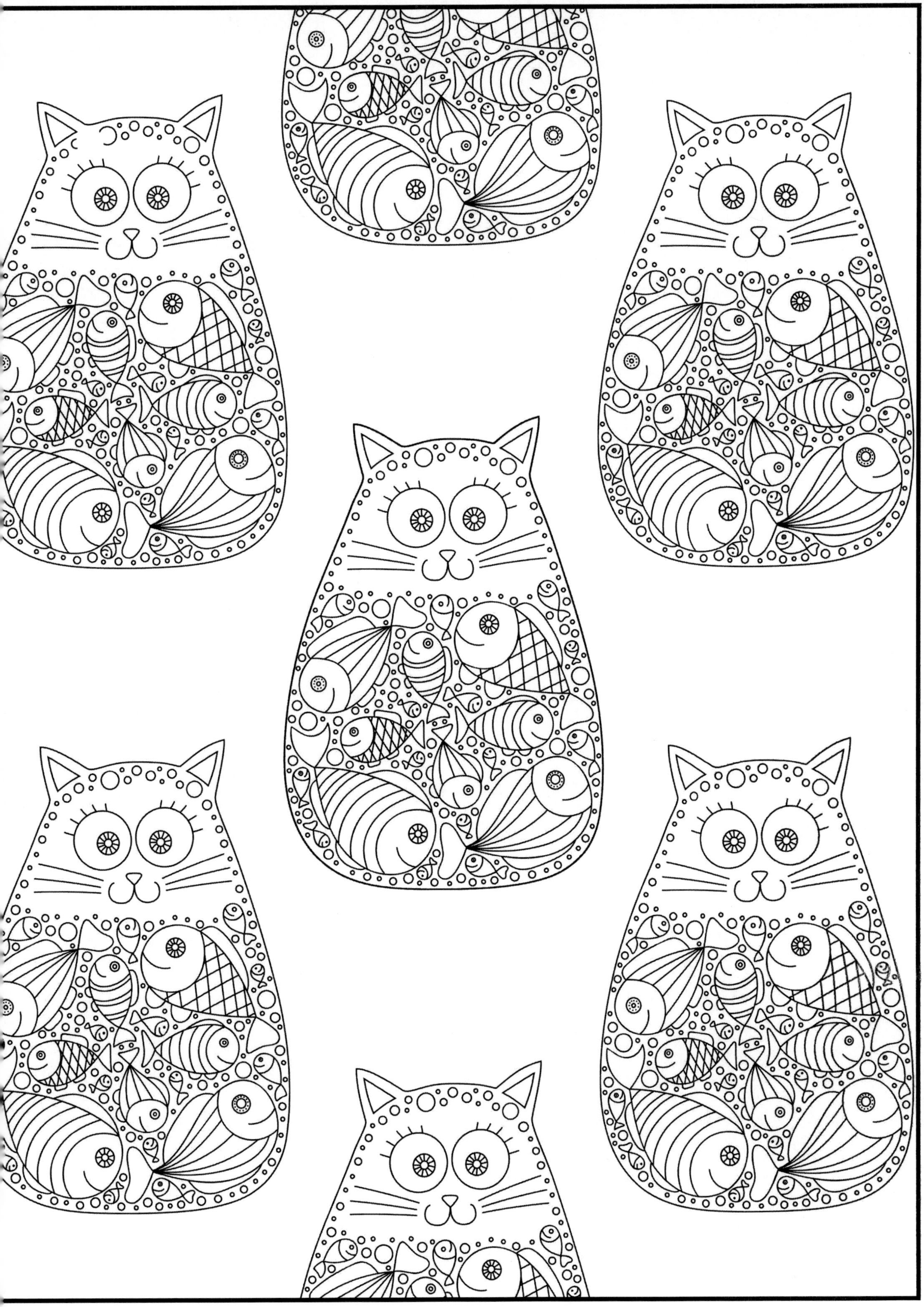

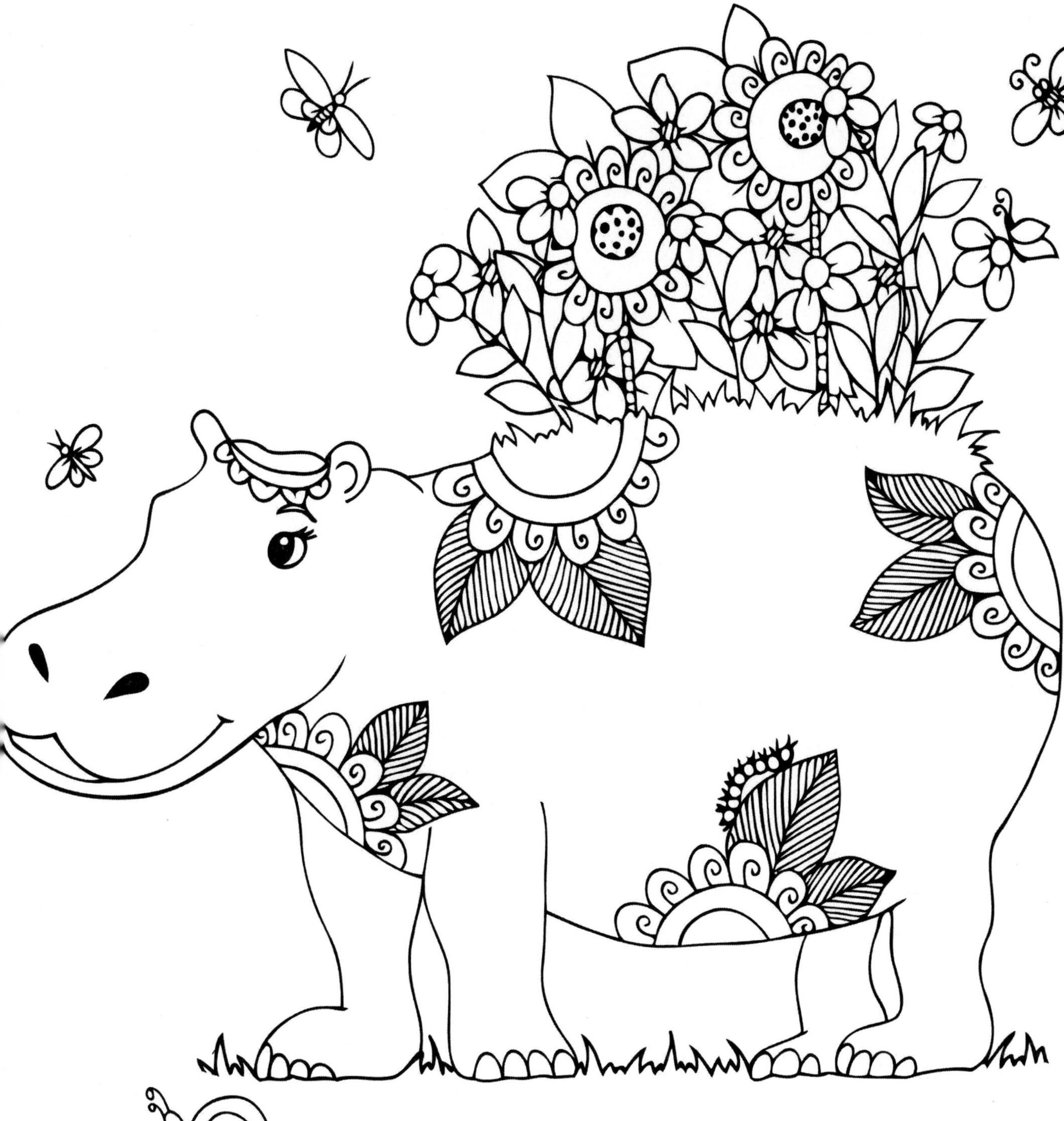

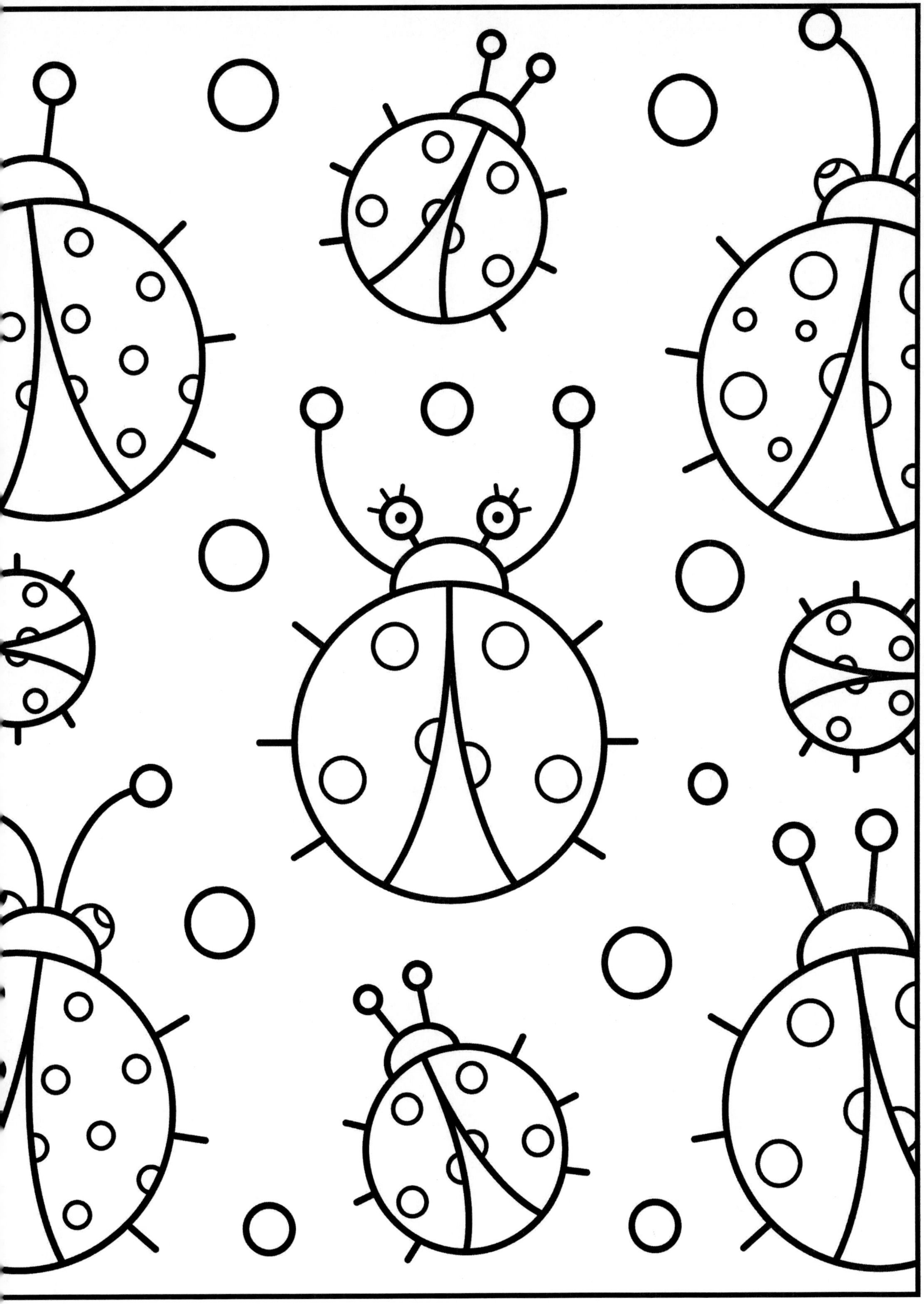

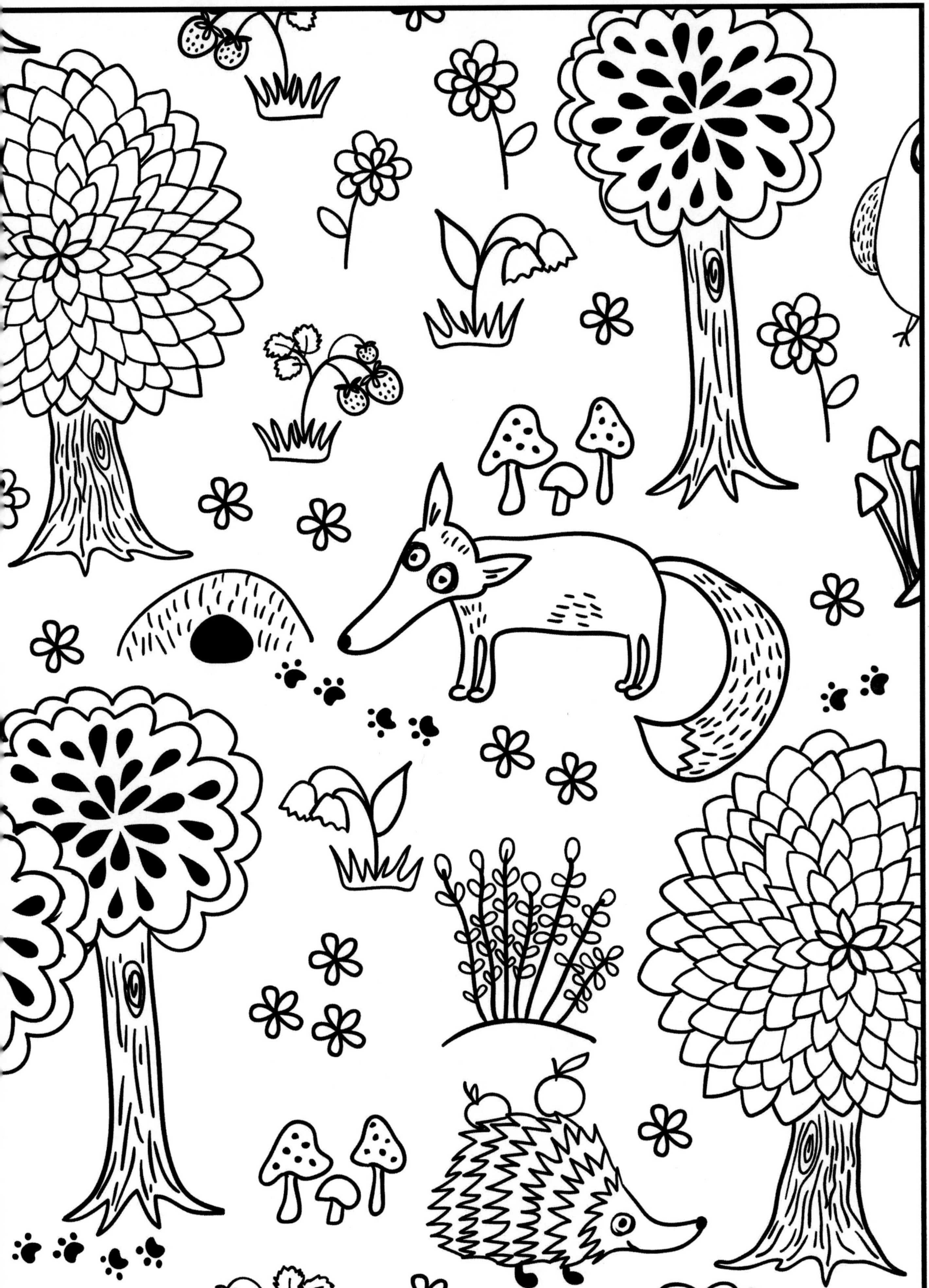

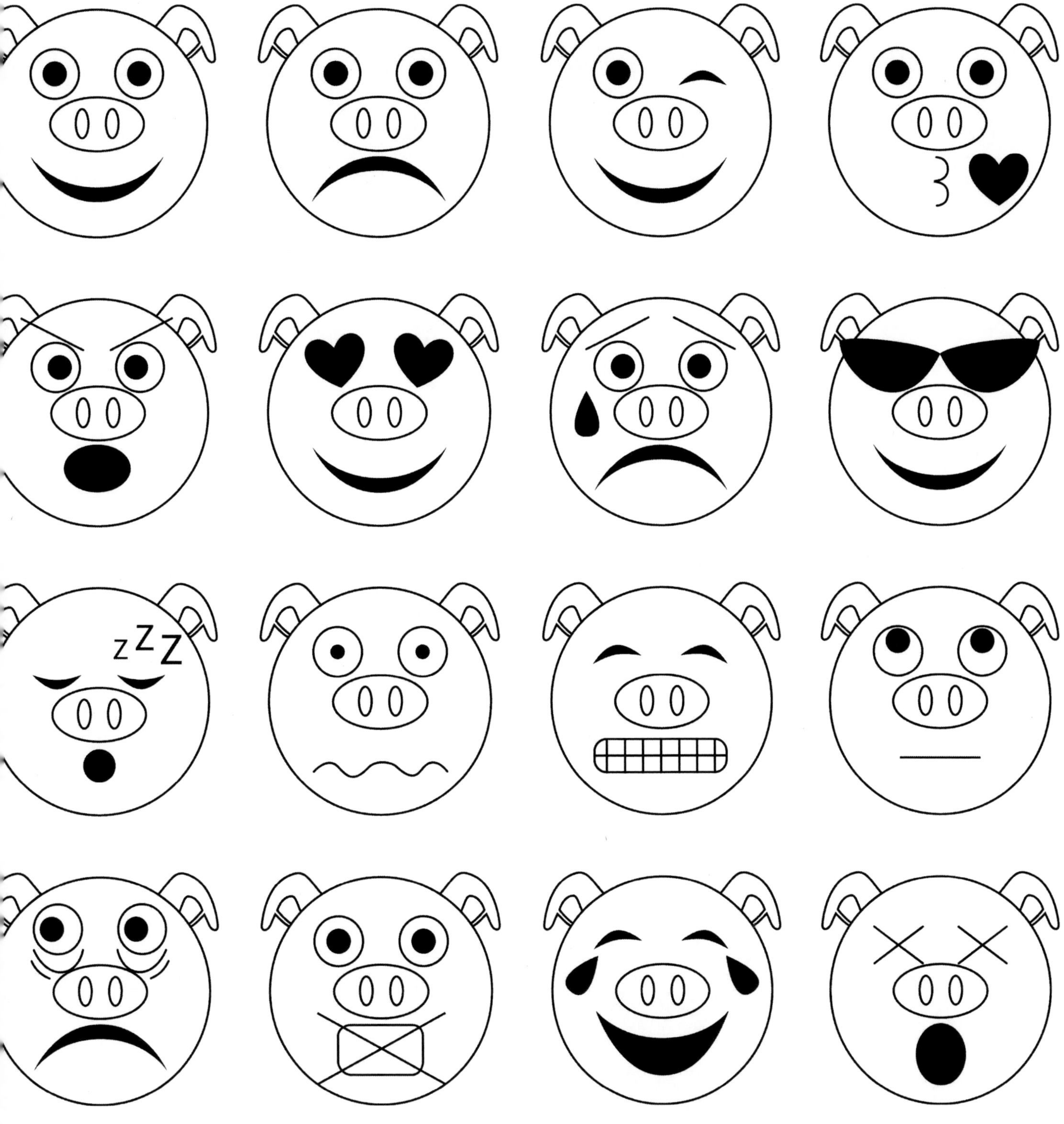
zZZ

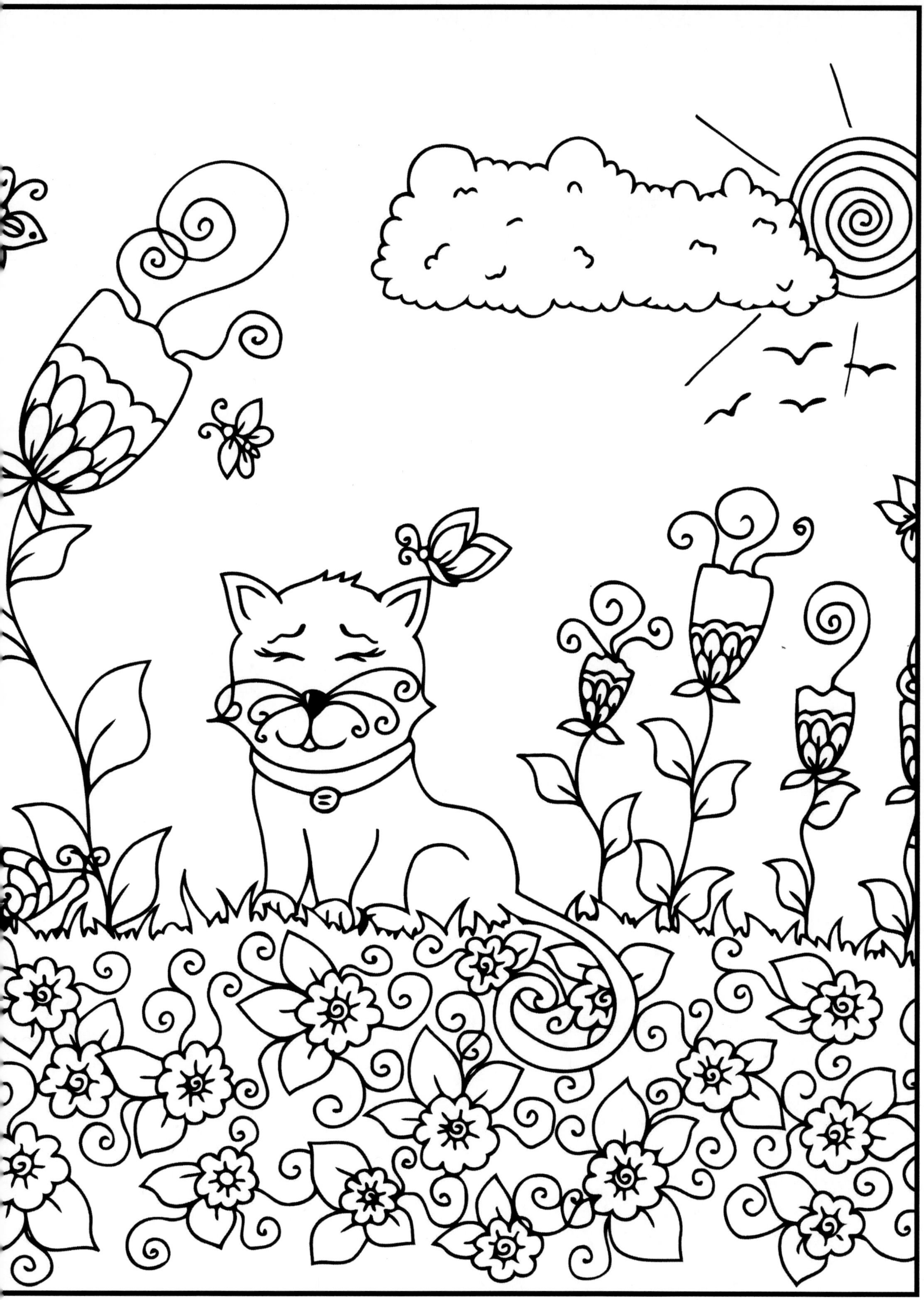

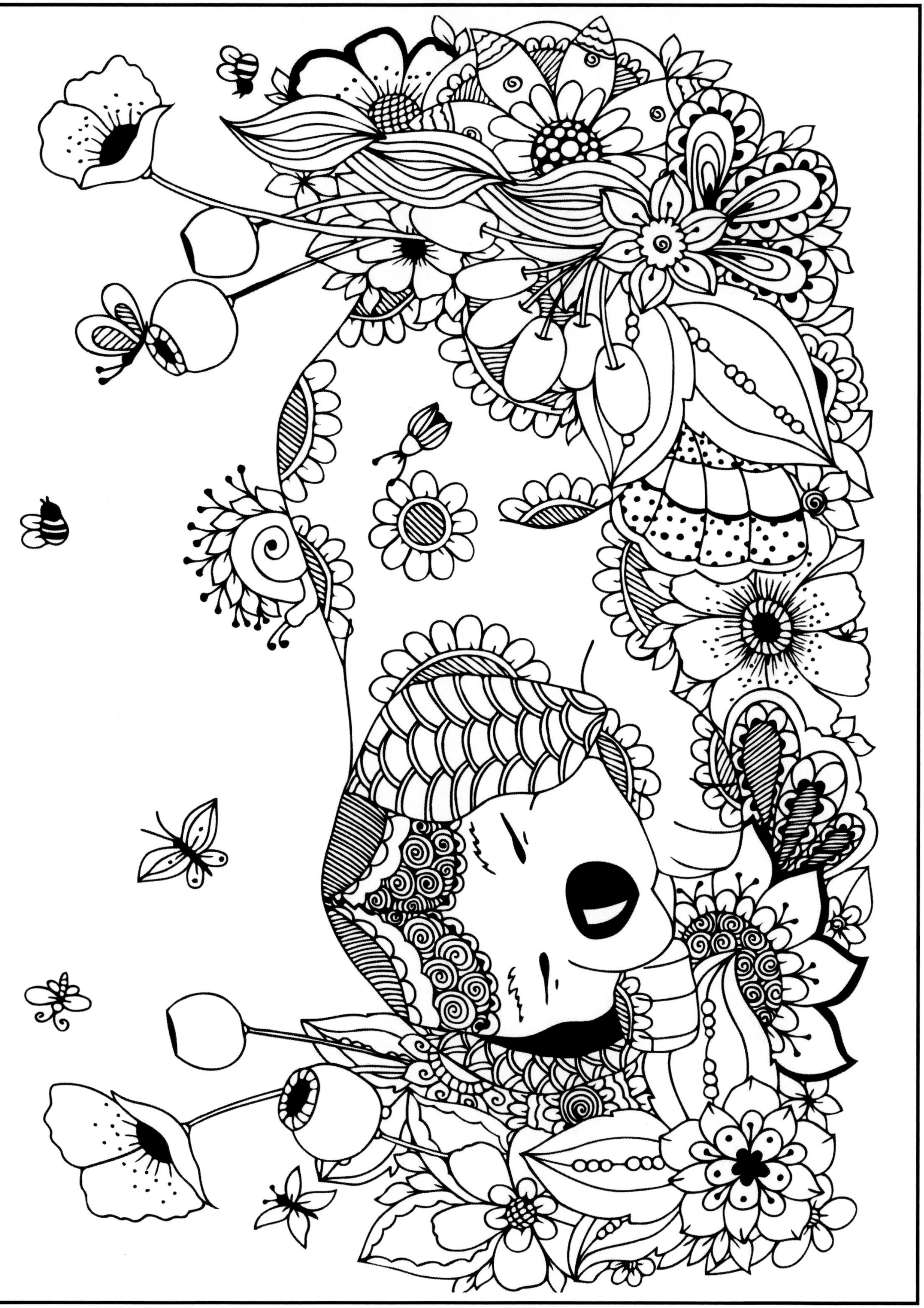

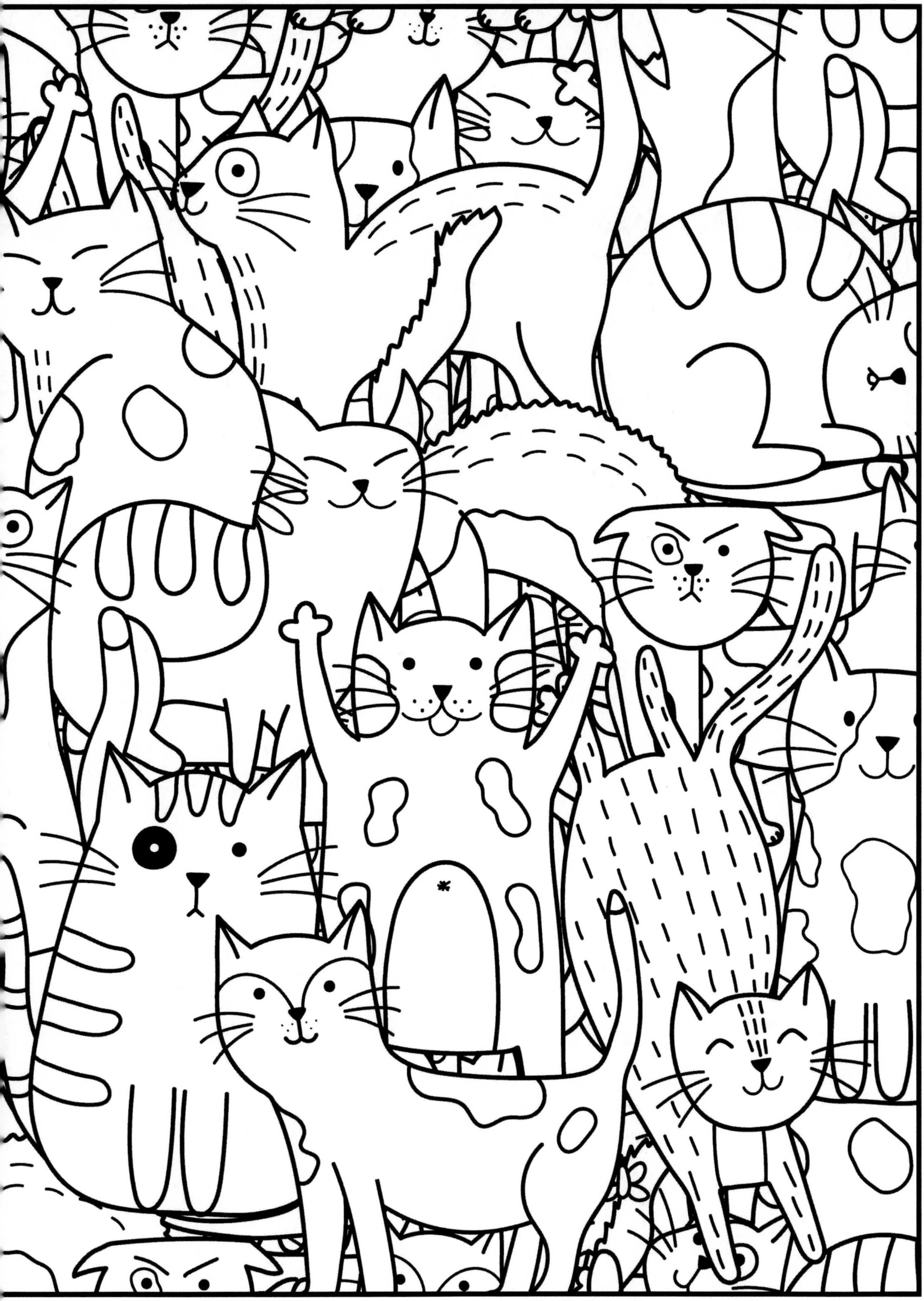

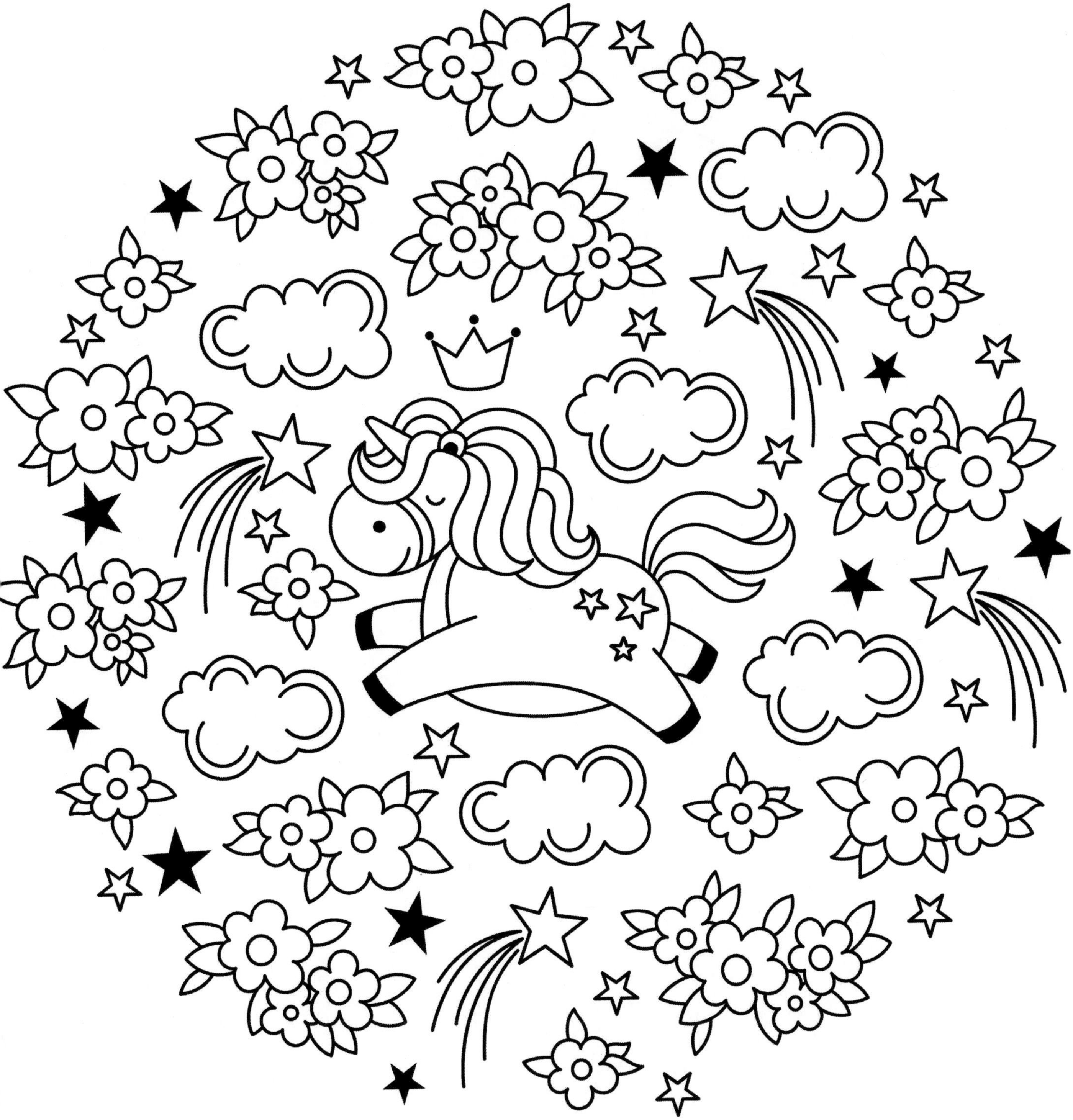

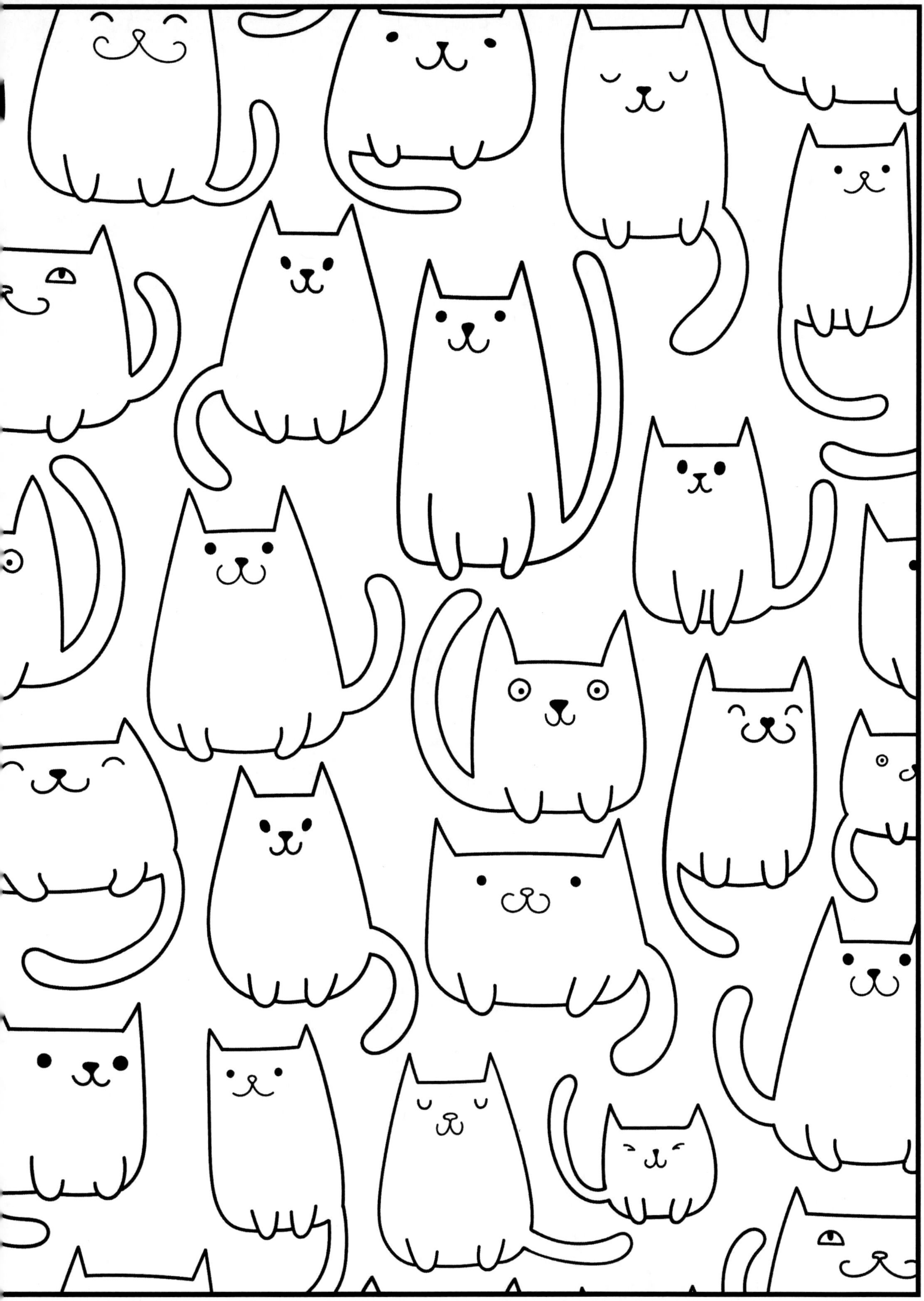

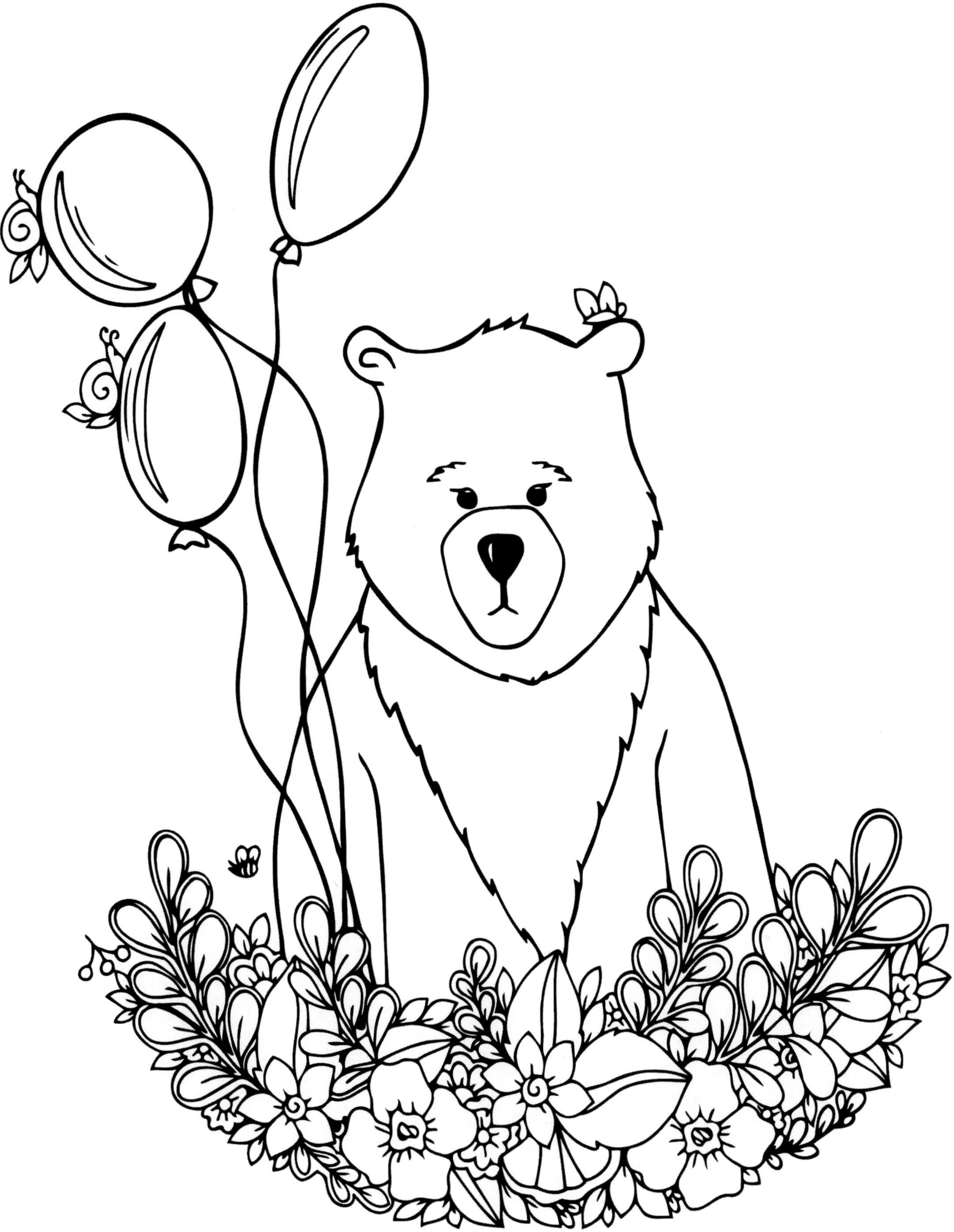

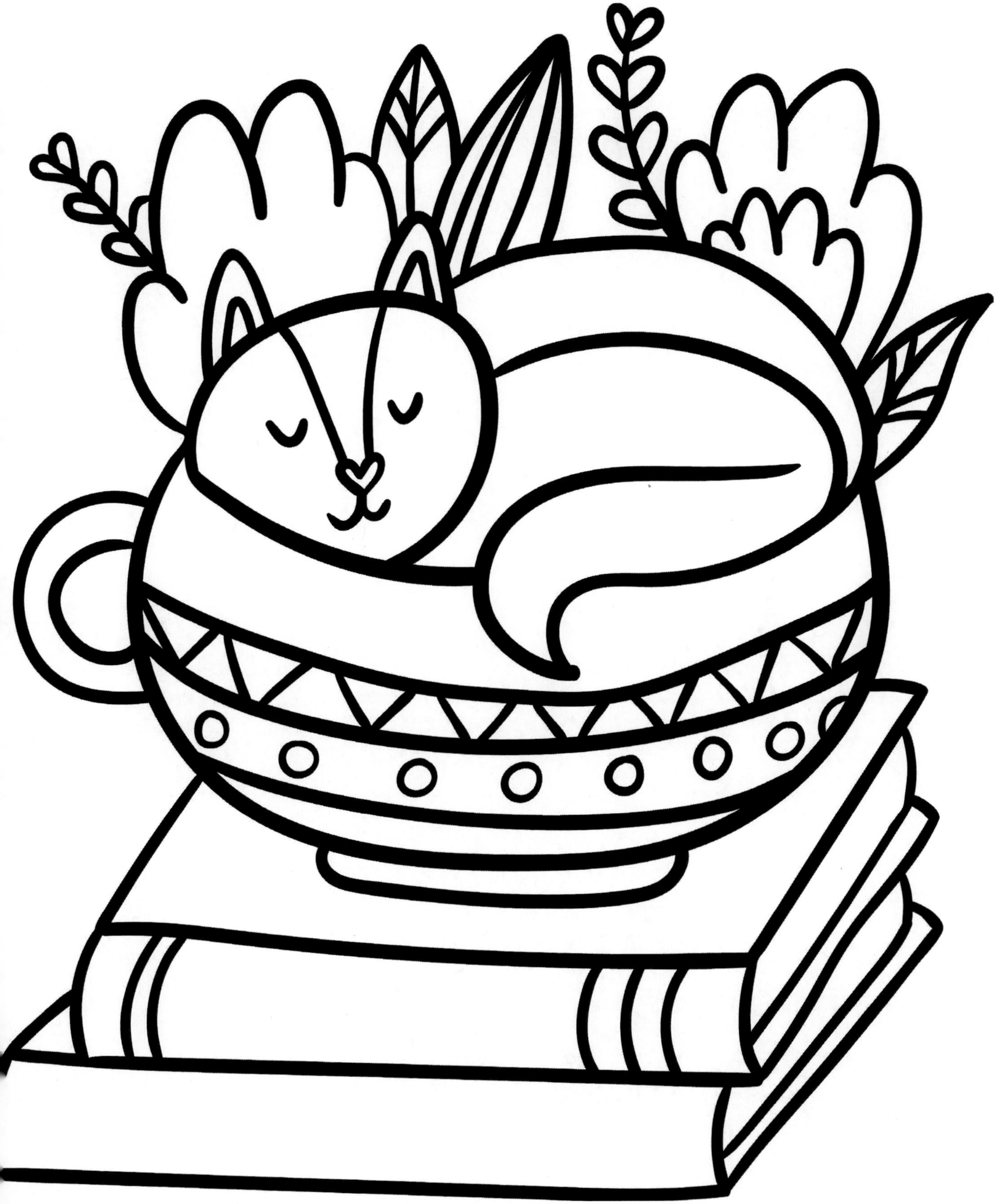

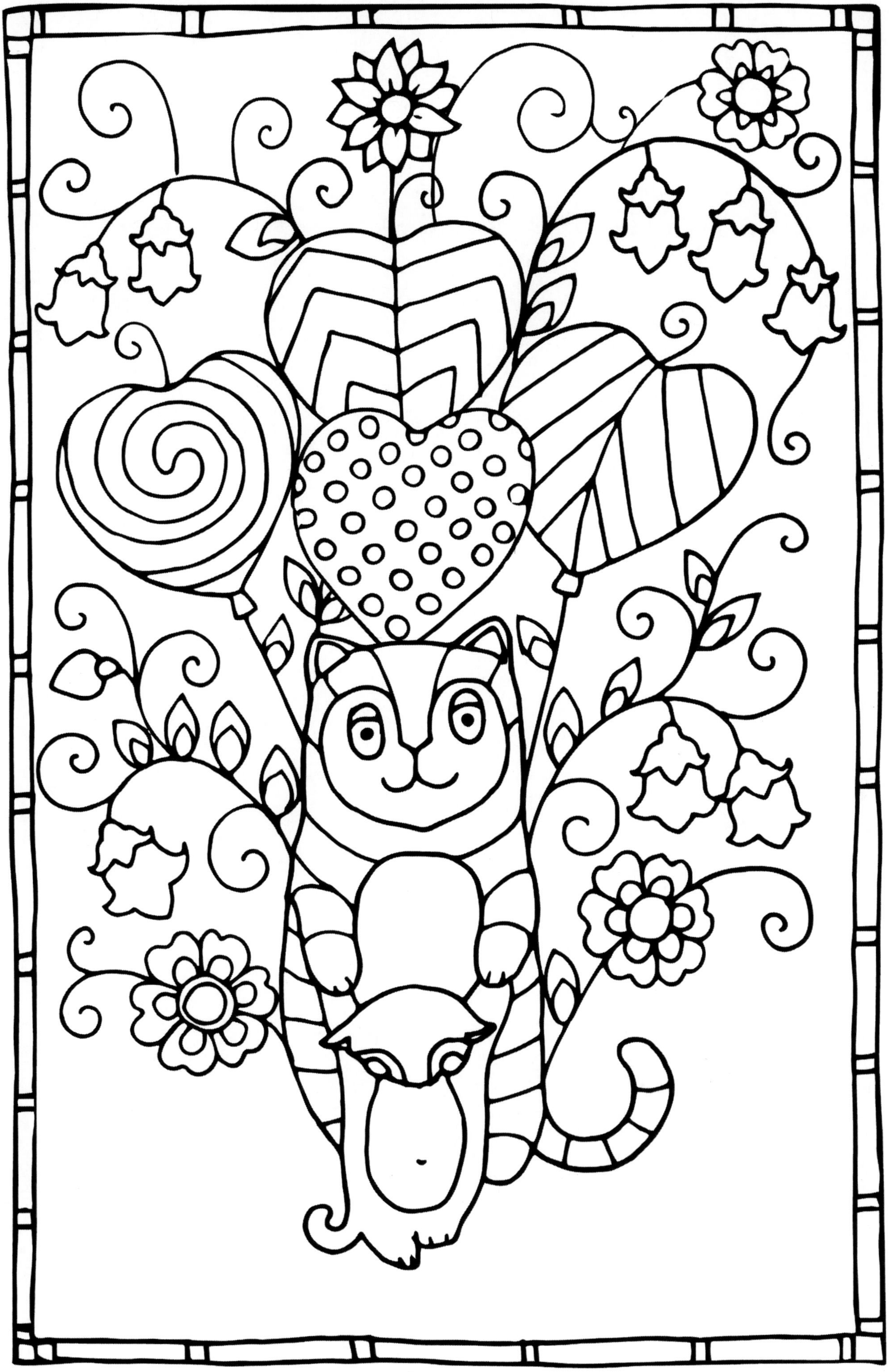

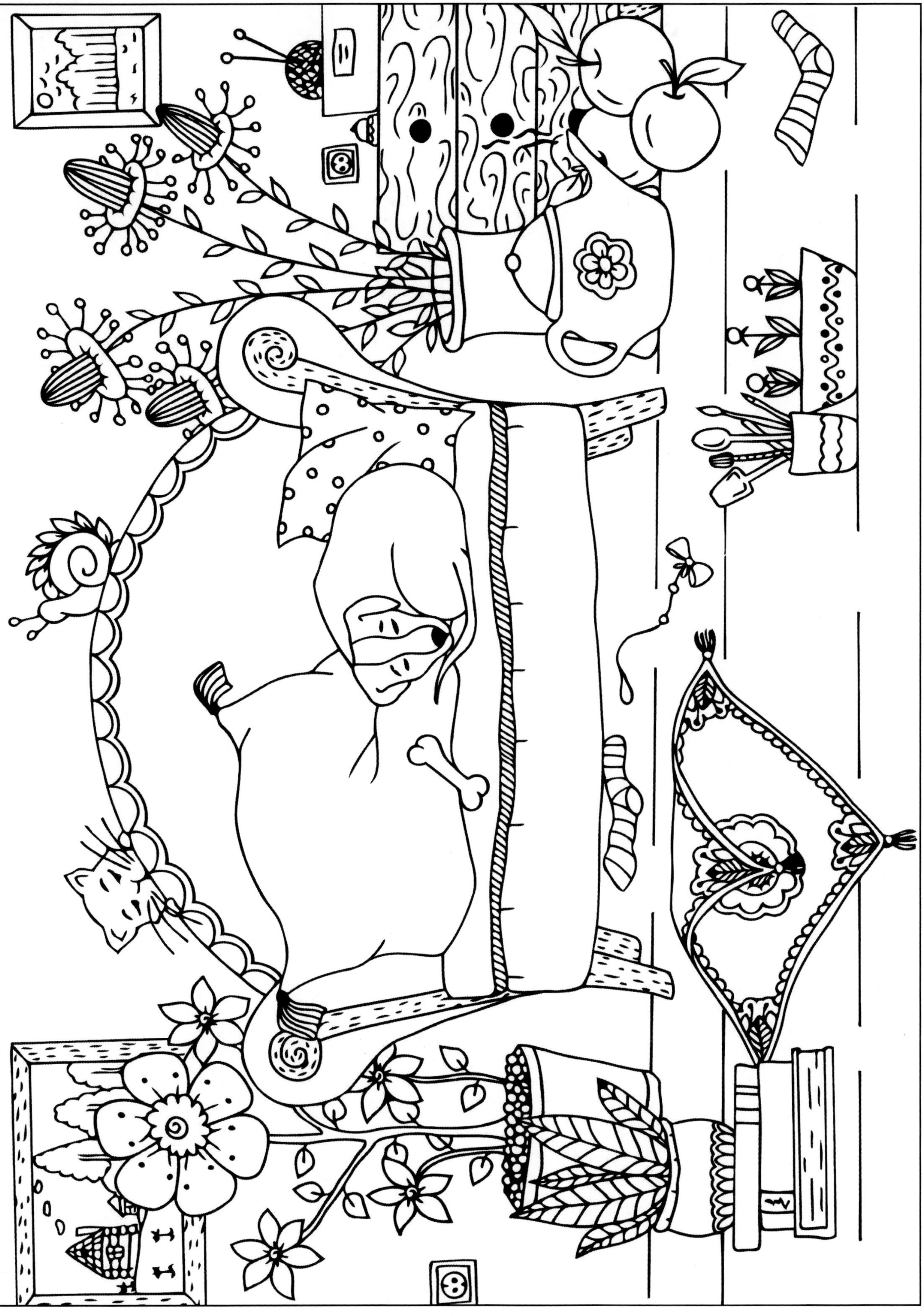

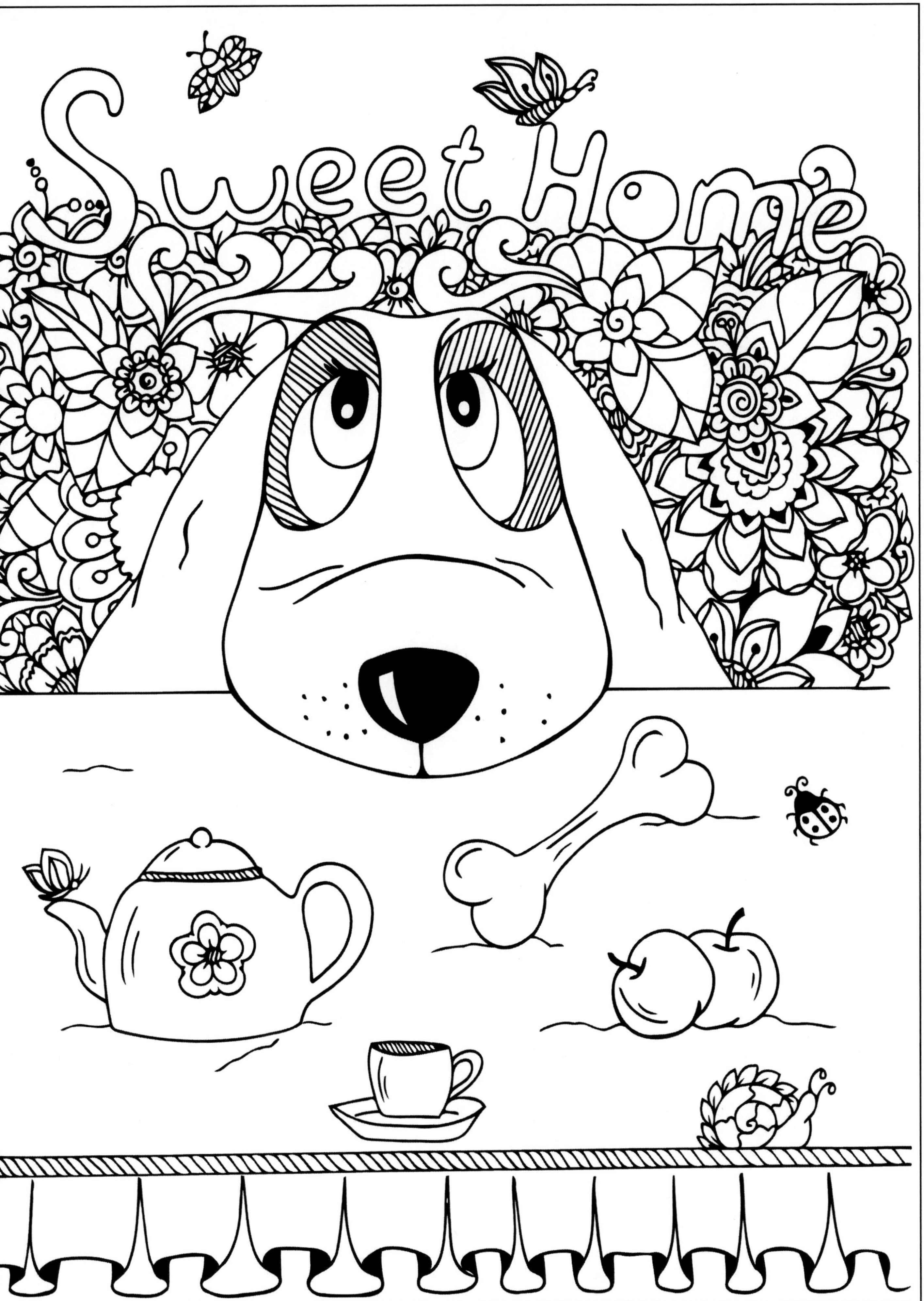
Sweet Home

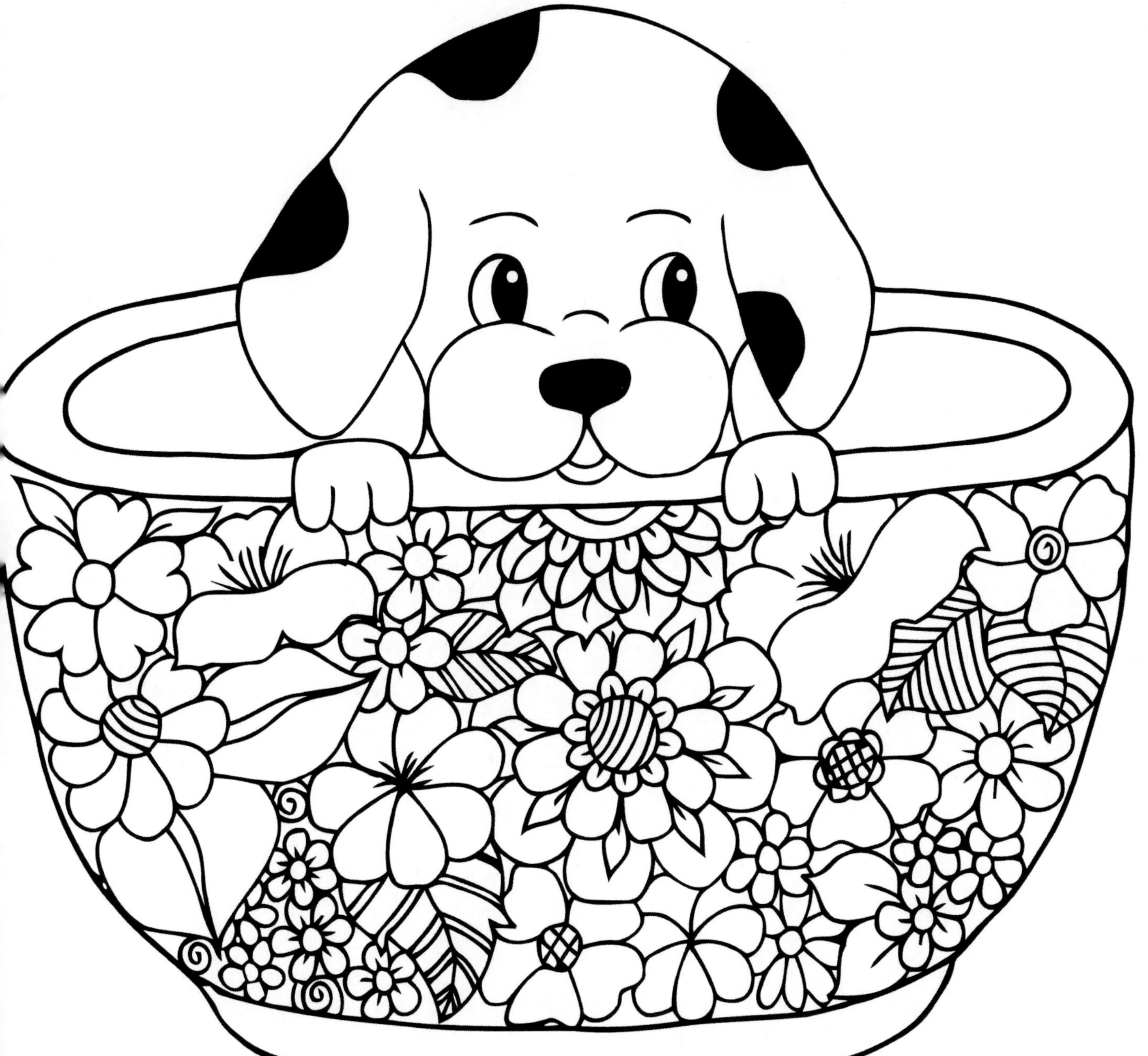

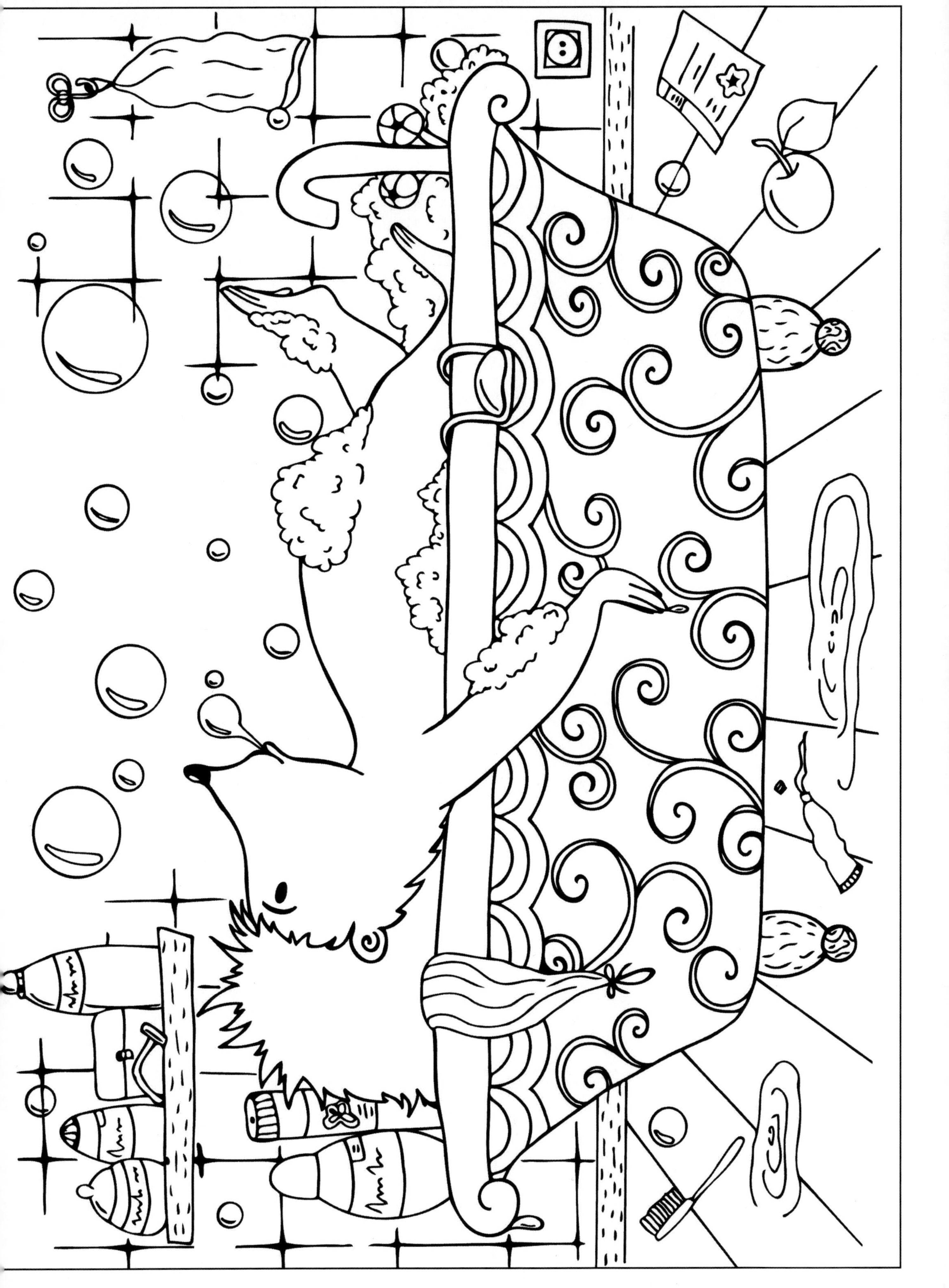

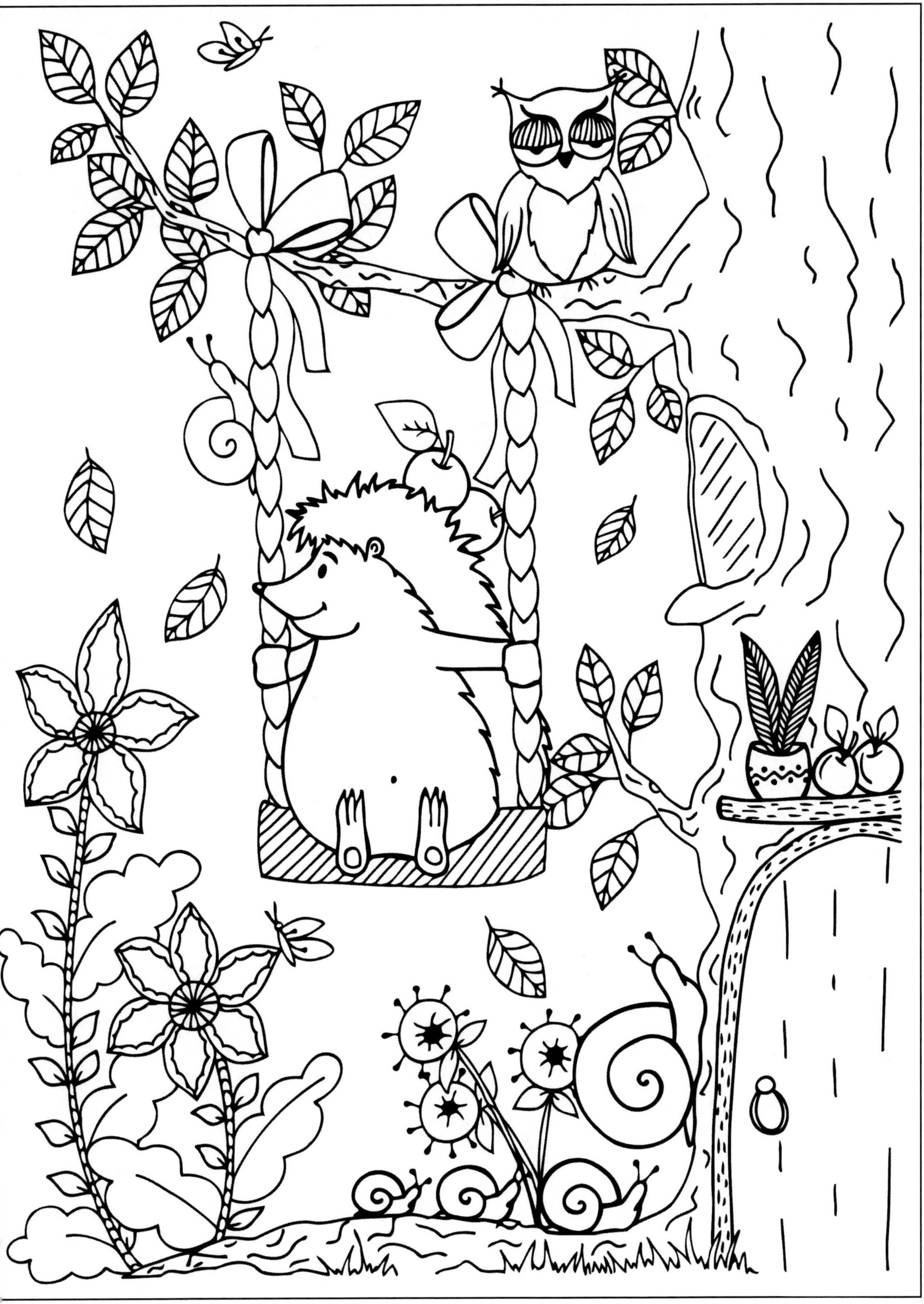

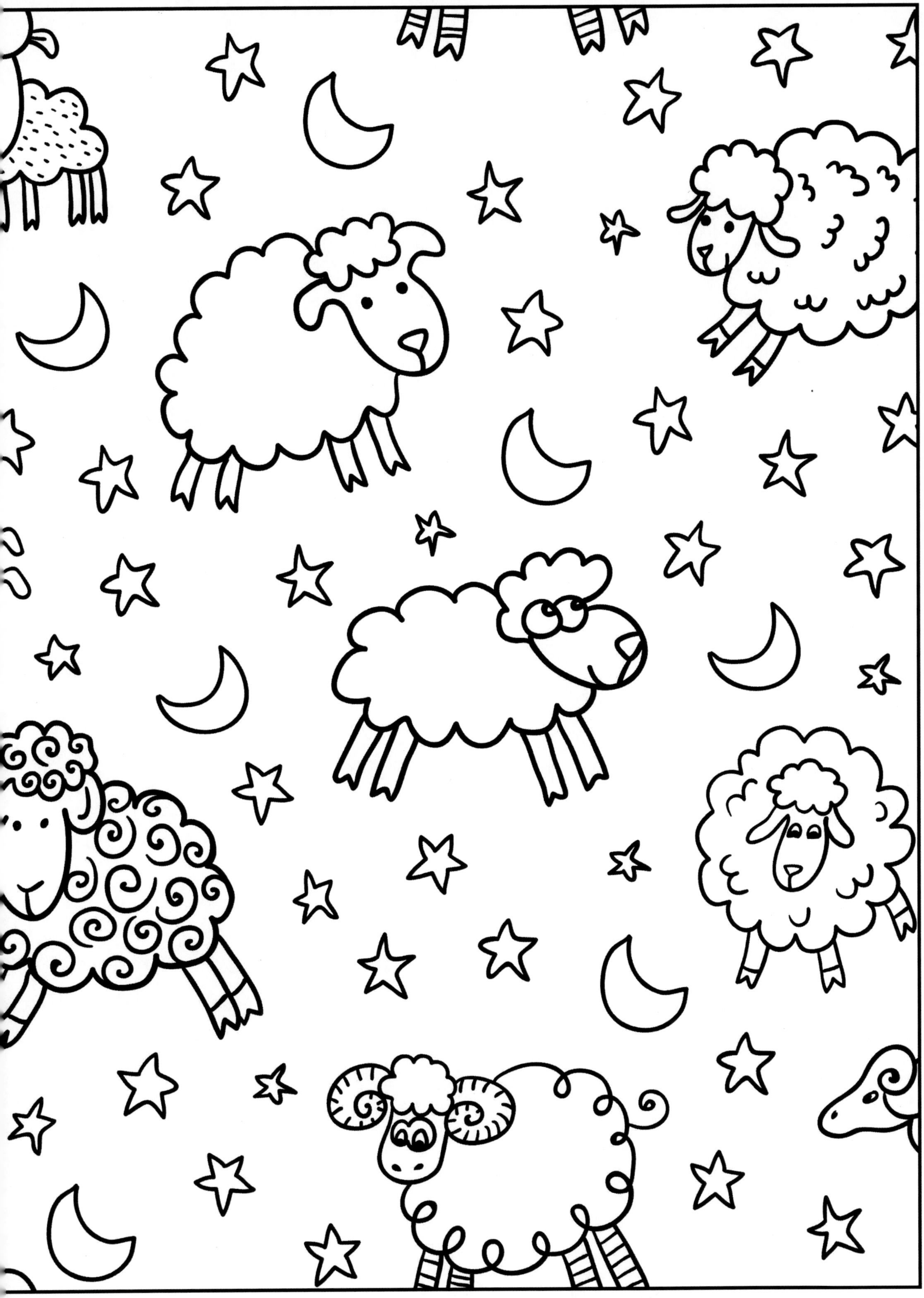

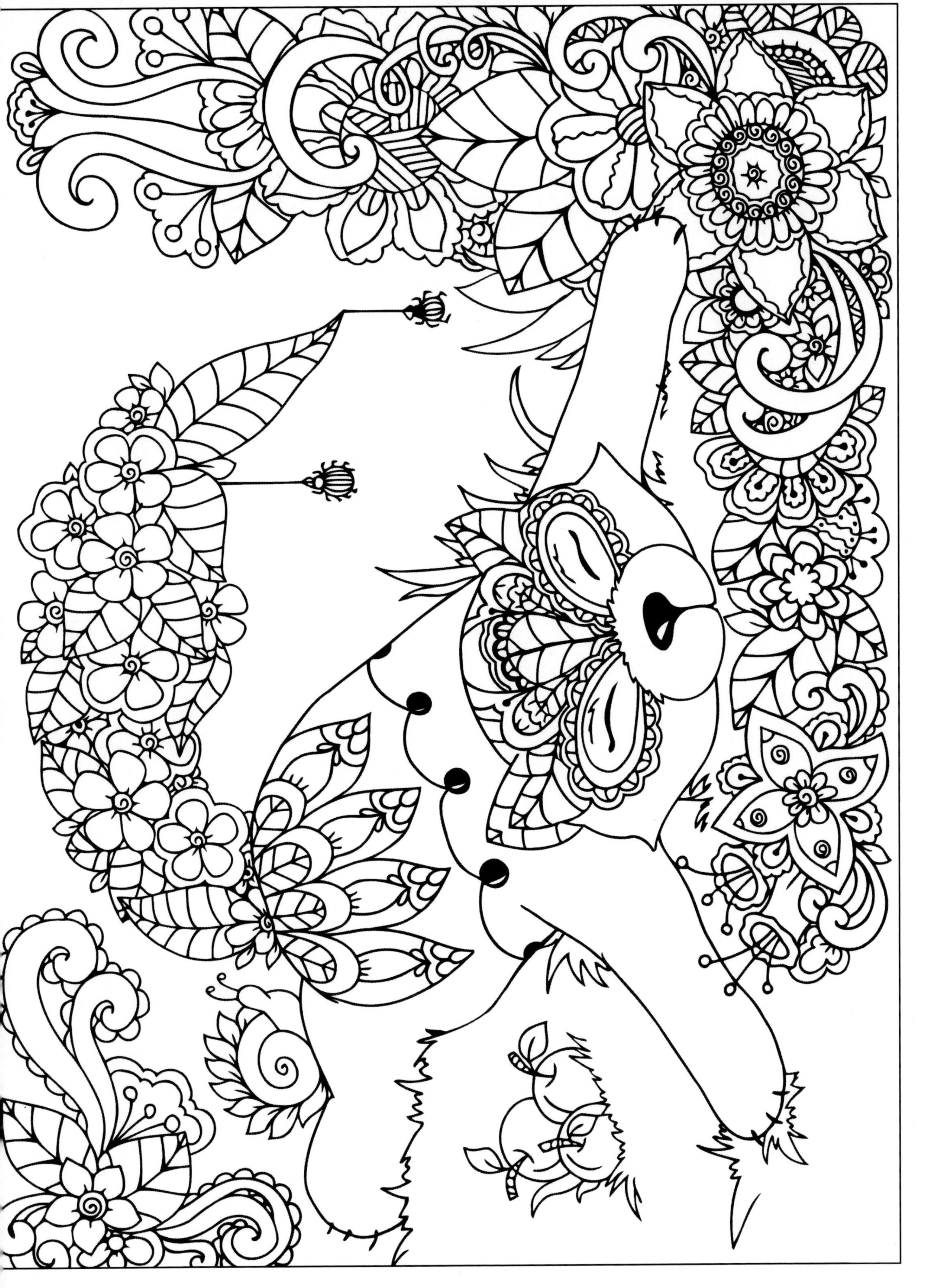

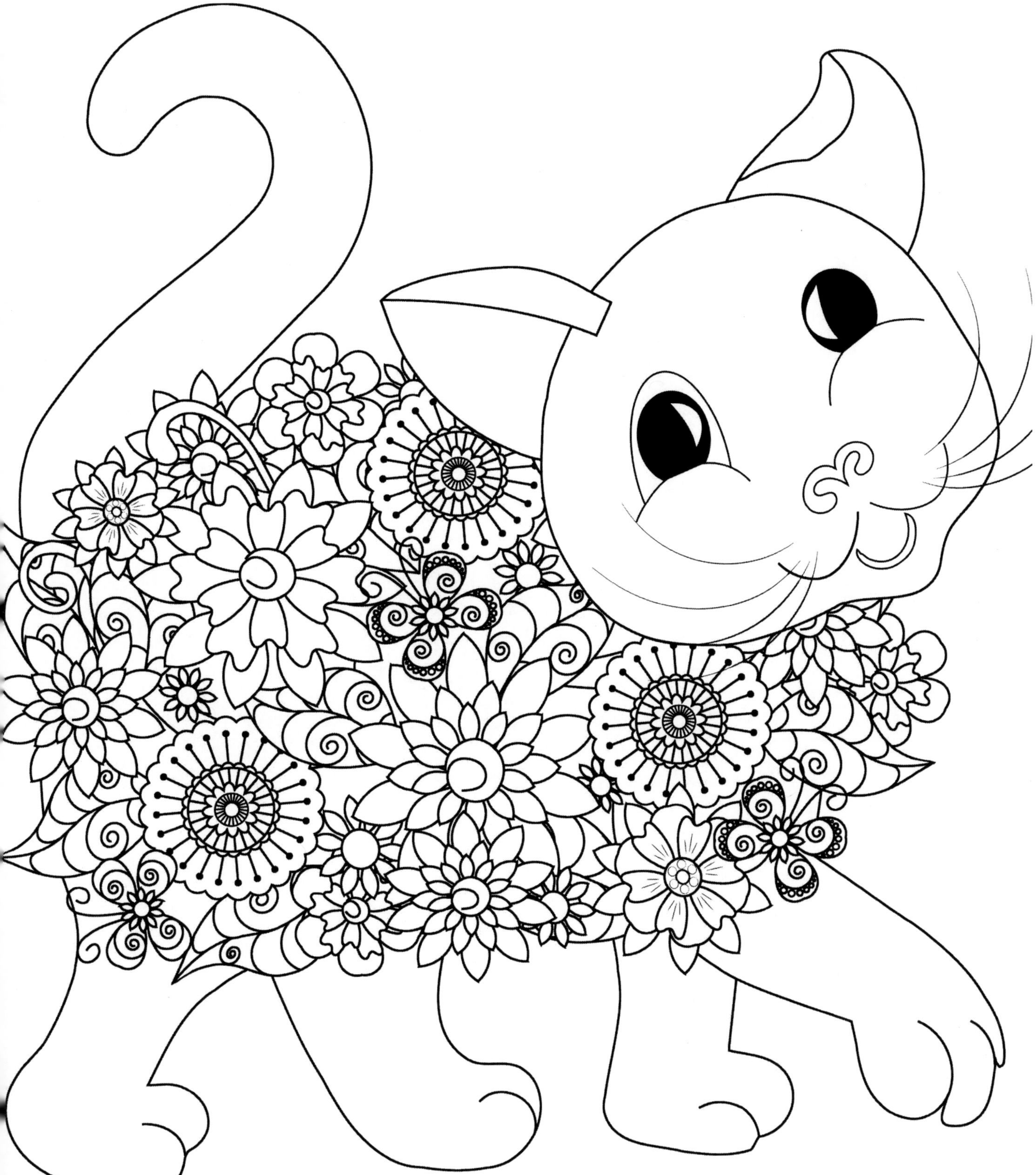

Made in United States
North Haven, CT
13 March 2023

34019444R00043